# Safonfok, Kosrae: Emergence of Complexity

## An archaeological investigation of prehistoric settlement in East Micronesia

## Felicia Beardsley

BAR International Series 1366
2005

Published in 2016 by
BAR Publishing, Oxford

BAR International Series 1366

*Safonfok, Kosrae: Emergence of Complexity*

ISBN 978 1 84171 808 8

BAR Publishing is the trading name of British Archaeological Reports (Oxford) Ltd.
British Archaeological Reports was first incorporated in 1974 to publish the BAR
Series, International and British. In 1992 Hadrian Books Ltd became part of the BAR
group. This volume was originally published by Archaeopress in conjunction with
British Archaeological Reports (Oxford) Ltd / Hadrian Books Ltd, the Series principal
publisher, in 2005. This present volume is published by BAR Publishing, 2016.

Printed in England

# BAR
PUBLISHING

BAR titles are available from:

BAR Publishing
122 Banbury Rd, Oxford, OX2 7BP, UK
EMAIL    info@barpublishing.com
PHONE    +44 (0)1865 310431
FAX    +44 (0)1865 316916
www.barpublishing.com

# SAFONFOK KOSRAE

## emergence of complexity

"All the past is but the beginning of a beginning."

H.G. Wells[1]

[1] From his 24 January 1902 lecture 'Discovery of the Future' presented at the Royal Institution in London and reprinted in full in the journal *Nature*.

A number of people have directly contributed to the success of the project work, none of which would have been possible without their unwavering involvement. The first is Mr. Berlin Sigrah, Kosrae's Historic Preservation Officer, whose offices are responsible for facilitating and sponsoring the fieldwork. Dr. Felicia Beardsley, University of California, served as principal investigator, and planned and directed the field and laboratory work as well as facilitated the analyses and other post-fieldwork necessities. Mr. Standon Andrew and Mr. Nena Lonno, both from the Kosrae Office of History and Culture Preservation, served as field directors, often doing double duty as laboratory supervisors and logistics negotiators for goods and services needed over the course of fieldwork.

Each season's crew consisted of local, hand-picked men, all of whom worked the full length of the project and, though archaeological neophytes, completed all work with the full complement of professionalism usually exhibited only by the most seasoned archaeologists. Here, the needs of the HPO were directed toward one goal: prepare and train a cadre of local men across the island who can be called upon to assist in future archaeological and historical projects. The 1999 crew was selected from a host of young men in Malem; the 2001 crew were local men from Walung. In 2001, historic preservation staff members from the Marshall Islands, Yap and Chuuk joined the project as a way of honing their own field skills; each spent two to three weeks directly involved in the excavations, laboratory work and mapping. Three volunteers joined the project work in 1999; two volunteers assisted in the 2001 fieldwork. All project participants took part in the field laboratory, while special samples were sent to professional laboratories for identification and/or dating.

Funding for each season's work was provided by a grant from the U.S. National Park Service, Department of Interior, in partnership with the Kosrae Office of History and Culture Preservation. Paula Creech from NPS deserves special mention here, as she has been a constant advocate for archaeological fieldwork projects in Micronesia. Her enthusiasm and support is greatly appreciated. Of course, none of the work would have been possible were it not for the generous permission of the landowner, Mr. Stoney Taulung. To him, we all owe a debt of gratitude. He allowed us access to his land and the Safonfok site, and permitted us to stay in his house throughout the duration of the project.

It must be said that the contents, interpretations and opinions expressed in the following pages remain solely the responsibility of the author. They do not reflect the views or policies of either the U.S. Department of Interior, the Kosrae HPO, or any other person or agency. However, they have benefited from innumerable discussions with colleagues at various conference venues, with regional historic preservation staff members during subsequent archaeological training sessions and oral history workshops, with crew members during our fieldwork on other parts of the island (and the region), with Drs. Alan Hogg and Fiona Petchey at the Waikato Radiocarbon lab, with my students in the classroom, and at home with my husband and daughter. In fact, many additional thanks should be extended to my husband, Edward, for tweaking and editing the photographs and drawings included here—he didn't take them or draw them, I am responsible for that; his contribution has been in trying to make them presentable.

List of Crew Members, Participants and Volunteers:

1999 Crew:

Burdy Talley, Alik L. Sigrah, Swinger G. Charley, Junior K. Ittu, Yoshiro Abraham, Lyndon Andrew. Volunteers: Angunis Ned (Kosrae HPO), Kerrick Benjamin (Kosrae HPO), Lupalik Wesley (Kosrae HPO).

2001 Crew:

Hamlet Jim, Teye Taulung, Joseph Jonithan, Houver Alik, David E. Nena, Ridon Kilafwakun, Hemley Benjamin (Marshalls HPO), Fredrick Langmoir (Marshalls HPO), Arimichy Rudolph (Chuuk HPO), Anerit Mailo (Chuuk HPO), Stephen Mara (Yap HPO). Volunteers: H. Bruce Brandt (KVR), Gary Navarre (Kosrae HPO).

# CONTENTS

# I. INTRODUCTION

The following pages document two seasons of archaeological fieldwork at the site of Safonfok, a prehistoric monumental site on the southwest coast of Kosrae Island, Kosrae State, Federated States of Micronesia (Figure 1). In 1999 and then again in 2001, our fieldwork was conducted as part of an ongoing research and advanced field training program sponsored by the Kosrae Office of History and Culture Preservation. This program is one means by which office staff review, reinforce, augment, and expand their existing skills in excavation and interpretation, including strategies in map-making and archaeological survey, decision making in excavation, and methods in assessing the integrity and post-depositional condition of an archaeological site. Kosrae routinely extends this same program to other regional historic preservation offices, as well as the local community college, and other community organizations and government offices. This is, in part, one solution to the lack of available archaeological and historic conservation training programs in the region, where the sheer isolation of island nations and states scattered over vast distances of open water severely limits the kinds and numbers of professionally directed workshops, training programs and research opportunities in which historic offices and their partners can take part. So, when an opportunity arises, it is often opened to any and all in the region. In 2001, the Safonfok project hosted members of the historic preservation offices in Yap, Chuuk and the Marshall Islands, as well as local community members. All told, the results of both fieldwork and the concerted efforts of every participant on the project have led to the documentation of an extraordinary site.

For Safonfok, archaeology has served as the proverbial thin edge of a wedge, prying open a narrow window onto a neglected piece of traditional Kosrae history that has languished in the fog of an indeterminate past. Here, for the first time in the history of archaeological work on the island, a monumental site that was probably one of the few regional power brokers of its time has been recognized, documented and examined in detail. Safonfok, as it turns out, is one of a very few number of sites that contains a deep and extensive cultural deposit representing the daily activities of a high status administrative site. Its material culture assemblage has further disassociated the site from all others on-island, turning what is an already significant site into a singularly unique site and elevating it to the status of *type site*. Enshrouded in its cultural deposits is an entirely new artifact type—coral fishhooks—new to the island, to

the region and to the archaeological record of the Pacific generally. Thus far, this is the only archaeological site in the Pacific in which coral fishhooks have been observed, recovered and reported[1]. There are two earlier accounts of coral fishhooks in the Pacific archaeological literature, however, both recount oral testimony on the existence of such hooks, which describe these artifacts as ancient and primitive, and no longer in existence (Hedley 1896, Beasley 1928).

To say that Safonfok is an exceptional site in the historical inventory of Kosrae, and in the complex unwritten history of the island, is an understatement. On the surface, Safonfok could (and was) easily dismissed as a heavily disturbed site, abandoned and forgotten in the late culture history of the island. Its collapsed walls and disjointed structural foundations were nearly hidden in a dense tangle of jungled strand vegetation. To the surrounding community, it was a rich source of building materials and ideal habitat for land crabs. But, when the first spade of earth was turned over during our first season of archaeological exploration, this unknown, seemingly insignificant site was transformed into one of the most distinctive and important sites on the island and in the region.

Below the ground was a virtually intact cultural deposit that recounted a silent history of wealth and extravagance within a political center that also maintained control over the production of such precious commodities as canoes, adzes and beads. Above the ground, the foundations of the walls and buildings described a fortified compound, complete with canoe landings, formal and informal entries, a market or distribution center, guest housing, and even the quarters of a specialist in medicine. Dates from the excavations suggest that the compound was continuously occupied from at least A.D. 1200 to 1600, a formative period in the history of Kosrae where social, economic and political forces around the island were negotiating for status, position and power, especially power. At stake was control over the flow of people and resources, goods and services throughout the polities on the island; expansion of the island's influence beyond its shorelines; and mastery of the oceans and islands throughout this part of the central Pacific. Legendary

---

[1] In 2002, I recovered two coral fishhooks from buried prehistoric era cultural deposits on Kwajalein Islet, Kwajalein Atoll, Republic of the Marshall Islands. This is the first recorded instance of their presence in the archaeological record of that archipelago.

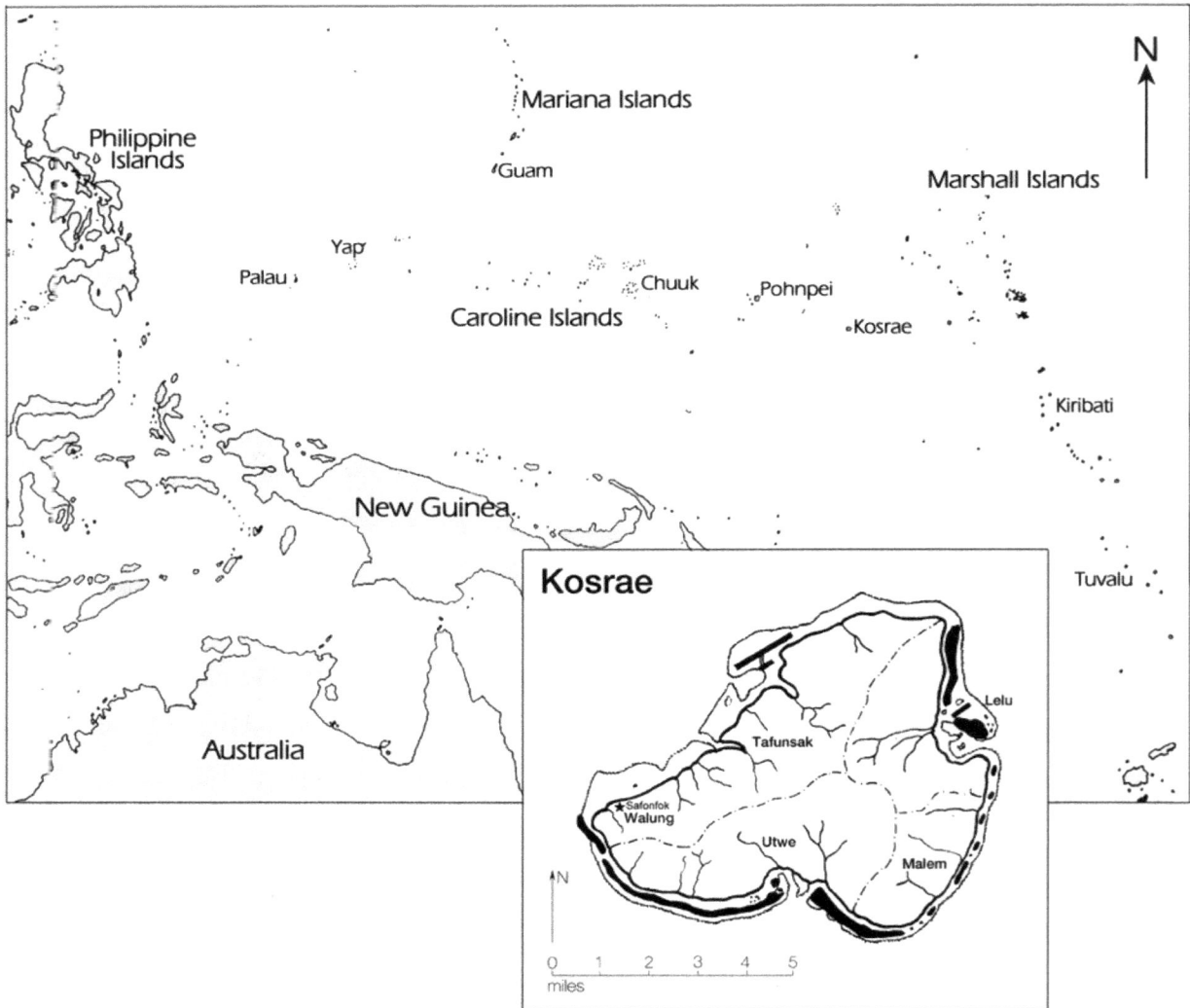

Figure 1. Map of Micronesia and the Western Pacific with an insert showing Kosrae and the location of Safonfok.

histories allude to Kosrae's extra-island influence, dominance and even intervention in the political affairs of the distant islands of Pohnpei and Chuuk. These same histories also hint of a period of unrest before final unification of the island under a single, paramount chief. But none of these histories are recorded in any detail; we are left only with suppositions, mere hints at possible scenarios. The excavations at Safonfok have raised a number of questions about this distant time, with one main question dwarfing all others: did Safonfok play a definitive role in these events?

Ground reconnaissance, intensive survey and data recovery excavations were the principal activities of the Safonfok archaeological fieldwork. Basic laboratory analysis and the production of a detailed site map were also integrated into the overall scope of project work during each field season, although they remained

secondary to actual data collection. Only a small portion of the site was systematically excavated and sampled over the course of our two field seasons, with a total of 27.9 square meters opened (0.32% of the site area) and 14.3 cubic meters of sediments examined. Concurrent to the 2001 excavations, a detailed site map with 820 mapping points was produced. Specialized samples of charcoal and midden were extracted from the excavations, along with the recovery of a number of indigenous, prehistoric era artifacts and refuse from traditional manufacturing industries. Next to the coral fishhooks, unique coral tools and shell bead types never before reported within the cultural inventory on the island were recovered, along with the full complement of debris derived from the production systems that accompanies each of these artifact types. Several earth ovens were exposed over the course of excavations, along with a buried coral pavement, a shell fishhook (the

2

first recovery of such an artifact outside Leluh Islet), shell adzes and food scrapers, coral abraders, basalt knife fragments, a basalt sledge hammer, medicine grinding stone and basalt chopper, shell and stone flakes, coral and shell debitage, and fire-cracked rocks and coral.

The prospects of an even earlier, pre-A.D. 1200 occupation at Safonfok were raised by the enigmatic appearance of a leveled coral spread below the principal site deposit. This rather densely packed, bounded coral spread appears in only one small part of the site, on an interior portion of the raised back-beach deposit. Its appearance at the end of the 2001 field season prompted a number of questions, the first and foremost being, is this cultural or natural? Is this a remnant of an earlier human occupation? Does this represent an isolated, but extreme tidal surge event that inundated only this part of the site area and no other? Can such an event be correlated with other environmental data on sea level changes and major tidal events? The unexpected encounter with this feature raised the bar for field inquiries and improvisation within our field strategy for the site. Within the overall chronology of site development, the position of this feature remains unsettled although its origin does not. Its structure and composition appeared the likely product of cultural agents; its presence below the principal site deposit demonstrated an earlier human tenancy on this part of the coastline and in the site area. But, its actual placement in time is no more fixed than 'some time before the 13th century.'

## *The Report*

The technicalities of the research questions, field methods and laboratory analyses, along with the context of the archaeological work and an interpretation of our results are set forth in the following pages. All are aimed at evaluating the position of Safonfok in Kosrae's complex history of settlement, occupation and political-, social- and economic maneuverings. Each section of this report is focused on a specific part of the project research, beginning with the natural environmental setting of the site, a brief history of the recent cultural occupation and previous archaeological investigations on Kosrae. Section III presents the research objectives for the project and the methods by which they were to be addressed. Section IV consists of a detailed description of the fieldwork, including all sampling conducted through excavation and stratigraphic profiles. Section V presents the results of the laboratory analyses on the artifacts, midden material, and radiocarbon dating. Sections VI and VII are the concluding remarks, placing into context the significance of Safonfok within the historical record of Kosrae and the region.

It is hoped that the cumulative contribution of this investigation will launch a broader inquiry into the traditional, pre-Leluh history of Kosrae, with more attention and resources paid to those earlier eras leading up to the consolidation of power wielded by the hands of the paramountcy at Leluh. This was an important time in the history of Kosrae and other Pacific cultures. It was a time of expansion for the maritime powers throughout the region; populations were on the move over long distances, and short; posturing for position, power and prestige were the norm; intra- and interisland social, economic and political interactions were commonplace, with fleets of traders and empire-builders traversing the open waters between far-flung islands and within their own archipelagoes; ultimately, the trajectories of history converged to form powerful political centers controlled by an elite few, and built upon a consolidated and subjugated base of what once were independent states.

# II. BACKGROUND: SETTING THE CONTEXT

If we were to look at a map of the Central Pacific, we would be confronted with a region dominated by small coral islands, each resting low in the water and scattered along the edge of the Nauru Basin just like pearls loosed from a string. Kosrae is one of only three high islands in this part of the Pacific. It rests at the easternmost end of the Caroline Island arc, separated from the other two high islands, Pohnpei and Chuuk, by several hundred miles of open water and a sprinkling of low coral islands. To its south, east and north lay the linear coral clusters of the Marshalls, Kiribati and Tuvalu.

Located 5° north of the equator, the warm waters of the tropical ocean surround Kosrae and its narrow reef, a compound complex of both fringing and barrier reef. It is a small, isolated island roughly 42 square miles in area, with no outer islands of its own. Kosrae bears the roughly circular shape of a newly extinct oceanic volcano, but with a deeply eroded surface that reflects the ravages of time and a moist climate (Figure 2). Just over four million years ago, the island emerged from the deep recesses of the ocean, flowing from a hot spot on the descending edge of the Ontong Java Plateau, a small fragment of the Pacifica continent that splintered off the Gondwanaland supercontinent some 225 million years ago. The birth of this solitary island began like so many others, as a liquid mass of boiling magma issuing forth in successive eruptions, each cooled in turn by the ocean currents. As the burgeoning seamount grew and entered its subaerial phase of development, it had to pass through a final hydroexplosive zone that culminated in a cataclysmic episode of pyroclastic volcanism (Nunn 1994). A chaos of large talus slopes were created, followed by the formation of craggy recesses, toppled rock formations, large volcanic boulders, and a riot of landslides. In the final phase of island-building, oozing lavas armored the surface of this volcanic cone and, in essence, allowed it to persist as an island (Nunn 1994).

Jutting above the surface of the water, the tiny island of Kosrae greeted the world as a cluster of stark and barren black rocks soon to be populated by an assortment of lifeforms, including small spiders that floated in on strands of silken thread (Young 1999). They were joined by other species including a variety of microbes, spores, lichens and mosses, each of which set the stage for the arrival and colonization by still larger, more complex organisms such as ferns and flowers, then forests, insects, birds, bats, and reptiles. But no large animals or carnivorous beasts, until the arrival of the first human settlers. In the oceans, in the meantime, the coral reefs began to form, growing with the island and fluctuating sea levels. Fish, attracted to the coral, spawned and took up residence, as did other marine organisms; and in the blink of a geological eye, the waters were soon teaming with all variety of marine life (Young 1999).

It is this environment, a lush tropical forest supporting a rich and varied biota, upon which the founding human population took up residence at a time contested in history. It could have been 2,000 years ago, it could have been 2,500 years ago, it could have been even earlier. In any event, the first boats landed together with the fertile seeds of the complex civilization they were to become and set in motion a complicated sequence of events that ultimately led to the trajectory documented in historical records. It is a history complete with tales of domination, both of the natural world and the cultural, with expanding populations and settlement systems, the rise of local chiefs, regional and island alliances, and finally unification under the iron fist of a solitary leader. If there was a bastion of resistance on this tiny island, it too was brought into the fold at this time.

The history of Kosrae, its political and economic growth, the rise of administrative centers and power structures, and the ultimate unification of the island took place before the time of written records. It is a story that must be pieced together through fragments of legendary tales, oral histories and archaeological evidence. The following pages attempt to reconstruct a part of this story in one tiny corner of the island: Walung, the southwest section of the island said to be the initial landing site of the founding population and the likely place of the first settlements. We begin first with a description of the environment; afterall, settlement is a physical expression of the interaction of a culture and the landscape. To the distant eye, the island appears to be blanketed by a uniform tropical forest, yet there are distinct differences within this uniformity. These variations have influenced the course of cultural development, which in turn responded to, influenced and altered these environmental details in a complex, circular system of mutual feedback and induced modifications. Much of what follows is a basic description of the general environment of Kosrae, as we lack any in-depth or even rudimentary studies of the immediate environment or ecosystems in and around Walung.

Figure 2. *Sleeping Lady* profile of Kosrae's steep mountainous interior.

## Environment

Known as the "Gem of Micronesia," the emerald island of Kosrae was considered a remarkable exception in the middle of a sea of low coral islands. According to the early 19th century explorers (Ritter and Ritter 1982), this singular island was strategically located at the midway point in the shipping lanes between New Holland (Australia) and China. It provided a welcome respite with good anchorages, fresh water, food, and a generous and peaceful people. Throughout its history, in fact, it seems to have played a vital role as the gateway to Micronesia: it was the first high island encountered by ocean voyagers from the south in search of new lands to conquer and settle, new resources to exploit, new trading partners to cultivate, a welcome refuge from seasonal storms, and a place to rest and reprovision.

Its formation and history of environmental change is etched into the surface of its landforms. But, it is a history that is not easily read and remains sketchy at best. In general, studies of oceanic islands tend to be marginalized in the academic disciplines of the earth sciences and environmental studies, with very few studies of specific islands like Kosrae produced. These limitations and gaps in understanding the development and life cycle of an island are visible in the many assumptions about island formation, patterns of climate variability, distribution of vegetation and animal populations, even patterns of extinction; virtually all these assumptions are drawn from continental studies (Nunn 1994). Direct studies of islands, when they do occur, are often limited to economic resources rather than the condition of the overall environment. On Kosrae, many of the recent ecological and biogeographical investigations have focused on the mangroves as a principal contributory element to the economy of the island, and only secondarily as an indicator of the general health and integrity of the environment (Allen, Ewel and Jack 2001, Cole, Ewel and Devoe 1999, Devoe 1994, Devoe and Cole 1998, Drexler and Ewel 2001, Ewel et al. 1998, Ewel, Twilley and Ong 1998, Naylor and Drew

1998, USDA 1983). Beyond the mangrove systems, however, few (if any) detailed studies of the island environment have been undertaken. With the exception of these coastal studies, the overall state of knowledge about the island's environment does not seem to extend much beyond the observations of the first western explorers.

Reports on the pre-Contact/Contact environment come from a nearly continuous succession of historical accounts written at the beginning of the 19th century by the first western explorers to pass by and linger on the island (Ritter and Ritter 1982). Kosrae was one of the last islands in the Carolines to be explored by westerners, yet their accounts provide a comprehensive and detailed description of the island's natural and cultural environment; descriptions that are thorough in their approach and that appear to have directly benefited from the circumstances of late Contact. Previous accounts of Contact across the Pacific, recorded in the preceding centuries by generations of explorers and navigators, essentially laid the foundation for the more scientific observations of 19th century explorers, seamen, scholars, and naturalists (e.g., Wallace 1962). Gone were the fantastical and often romantic descriptions of initial encounters penned in centuries past; in their place were more matter-of-fact accounts rendered by a wiser, more experienced body of observers catering to a populace stirring under a new awareness of the world around them (Beardsley 1997b).

The first Western accounts of Kosrae describe an island with an imposing landscape, derived from an apparently simple and homogeneous geology. Here was an island with a steep, jagged mountainous interior shrouded in an almost impenetrable vegetation, abundant streams that tumble and crash from rock to rock until they slow to a meandering pace as they cross the alluvium of the coastal plain and eventually empty into the lagoon. The climate was murderously hot and humid; even the variety of flora and fauna was seen as nearly monotonous, with a prodigious and rampant vegetation covering the entire island. There were thick mangrove forests on the coastal margins, freshwater swamps, a narrow sandy strand, an abundance of springs and streams, and a permanently wet soil. The island supported a variety of both sea and land birds, small animals (rats, bats, lizards), a poor assortment of insects (though a large population of them), perhaps at least one large tree-climbing lizard, quite a few shellfish and fish, but no pigs and no dogs (Ritter and Ritter 1982). By all accounts, this was the stereotypical tropical island.

### Geology

Geology teaches us that land surfaces and the distribution of both landforms and water bodies slowly change and shift with time. As a consequence, the conditions encountered on an island today—the distribution of its landforms, the numbers and kinds of plants and animals present—do not necessarily reflect the conditions of millennia past. While it is not necessary at this point to say how these changes have taken place, we do need to recognize that such changes have occurred and are still occurring. From a geological perspective, Kosrae is an island in transition; it is continually evolving and changing along a course that will take it through the full cycle of birth, growth, reduction, subsidence, and eventual disappearance. This cycle was abruptly set into motion with the first eruptions from a rupture in the descending slope of the Ontong Java Plateau. At 4.2 million years ago, successive eruptions in the submarine environment created a solid basement of pillow lavas, sheet flow lavas and hyaloclastites (Sakamoto 1994). Labeled the Lower Volcanic Rocks layer, this was to be the first of four depositional episodes that characterize the island's geology. According to Nunn (1994), pillow lavas dominate in the initial upgrowth of seamounts generally; they are then followed by eruptions of clastics, which tend to concentrate on the flanks of the seamounts, forming sediment aprons and facilitating lateral expansion of the island mass.

As if following some unwritten geological text, the next, overlaying depositional episode in the Kosrae sequence, the Middle Volcanic Rock layer, is consistent with Nunn's (1994) basic observations of island formation. According to Sakamoto (1994), this next, overlaying depositional episode consists predominately of hyaloclastites, feeder dykes and, with the increased height of the seamount, sheet flow lavas. All three of these components contributed to the vertical and lateral growth of the island. Sakamoto (1994) dates this episode between 3.18 and 2.2 million years. As the burgeoning island enters the hydroexplosive zone, that is, that point near the sea surface where the explosiveness of underwater eruptions are no longer suppressed by the effects of water pressure (Nunn 1994), there is a shift in the materials incorporated into rock flows. This new phase appears to be dominated by sheet flow lavas, but there also appears to be considerable amounts of biogenic material such as corals and molluscan fossils coalesced into the mix (Sakamoto 1994). According to Nunn (1994), this eruptive phase also promotes the development of large talus slopes and the accumulation of clastic materials on the flanks and summits of the growing island.

The underwater eruptions must have ceased or at least slowed at this point in the island-building process, as there is a large gap in the dating sequence. It jumps from 2.2 million years at the upper portion of the Middle Volcanic Rock layer to 0.8 million years in the next overlaying layer, identified as Large Scale Intrusive Rocks and dominated by conglomerates (Sakamoto 1994). This transition period also marks a critical phase in the island-building process, the point where shallow underwater eruptions gradually shift to subaerial volcanism. Unless the eruptive material continues to

flow in equal or greater quantities, or the ocean water is blocked from the volcanic vents, the island is doomed to disappear (Nunn 1994). This is the point at which the island and its eruptive products are the most vulnerable to wave erosion, which often proves highly effective at removing any newly formed material, hindering island growth (Nunn 1994). By 0.8 million years, however, the island-building forces on Kosrae are once again at work. Lavas form the dominant eruptive products (Sakamoto 1994), increasing the vertical and lateral dimensions of the island. In the end, this will create a significantly different island in both its morphology and structure than its submarine predecessor (Nunn 1994).

The final depositional episode in the Kosrae sequence is the Upper Volcanic Rocks layer, dated between 0.72 and 0.5 million years (Sakamoto 1994). It is associated with massive sheet flows and the formation of sills and dykes. By the end of this depositional sequence, the island reached a new stage in its evolution. Volcanism ceased, either because the magma reservoir was emptied or redirected to another outlet, while other agents of landform sculpting took over.

As a newly extinct volcanic island, Kosrae seems to have taken on the generally circular shape of other such islands that enter this new stage of metamorphosis with a parasol-like, radial pattern of drainages (Nunn 1994). The events and agents of change from this point forward can only be speculative, drawn from descriptions of other, similar volcanic islands that exhibit high elevations and a high annual rainfall (Nunn 1994). Erosion is one of the key agents of change, however, influencing rates of denudation, river downcutting, chemical weathering, mass wasting, and even soil avalanching. With time, the tidy pattern of radial drainages becomes less distinct, with non-radial elements developing in a shifting landscape. Headward extension of some streams, for example, result in the capture of the headwaters of other drainages (Nunn 1994). Planezes or interfluvial plateaus form on the lower slopes between principal drainage outlets, while high cliffs along coastal exposures remain vulnerable to marine erosion.

Eventually the planezes are cut by erosional forces, leaving a landscape dominated by a series of relatively radial valleys separated by sharp, serrated interfluves that converge onto the rims of old volcanoes (Nunn 1994). Amphitheater-headed valleys take shape in the headwaters regions of some drainages and tend to display a distinctive shape: commonly broad in their upper reaches, narrowing to gorges downstream. Continued erosion usually cuts down the walls of these valleys and eventually breaches the interfluvial boundaries (Nunn 1994). In the final stages of erosion, the skeleton of the volcanic island core is exposed, leaving such prominent features in the landscape as volcanic necks and dykes; a jaggedy landscape that gives every appearance of melting into the surrounding ocean.

Where Kosrae stands in this evolutionary sequence is a topic for discussions that border on the rhetorical. Some may look at the jagged, sharp interior ridgeline and its steep sweep to a shallow alluvial plain on the coastal fringe and declare firmly and resolutely that the island has entered the late stages of its evolution. Others may see the island as relatively young, still in an active period of erosional sculpting. In the continuum of changes, however, such modifications are taking place within a geological time scale, where human experience and settlement amounts to less than 0.5% of the time since the last island-building volcanic eruptions. Our own experience within the geological life span of the island, then, is limited, very limited. We are met with an island where several mountain peaks reach elevations of 600 meters above mean sea level; where these same peaks and ridges capture passing clouds that ultimately influence the orographic contribution to the climate; where nearly 70% of the island is comprised of mountains, with another 15% tied up in foot slopes and alluvial fans, and the final 15% dominated by mangrove swamps and the coastal strand (USDA 1983).

The reef surrounding Kosrae is also geologically young, much like its host landform. It is a thick belt of coral, according to Lesson (Ritter and Ritter 1982), that encompasses a narrow lagoon and consists of a fringing reef that merges with short spans of a barrier reef. The reef is broken in four places, each of which corresponds to the outlets of major rivers. Natural bays or harbors formed at these river mouths and serve as the island's principal anchorages. Innem, Tofol and Tafeyot Rivers merge to empty into Leluh Bay, referred to as Charbol Harbor by western explorers; Utwe and Finkol Rivers ultimately empty into Utwe Bay, historically referred to as Lottin Harbor; Okat River empties into Okat Bay, referred to as Coquille Harbor in historical records; and Yela River empties into Yela Bay, identified on historical maps as Berard Harbor (Cordy 1993; Ritter and Ritter 1982). Just inside the lagoon, short sections of a remnant raised reef platform bespeak of higher sea levels in the past, possibly coincident with the mid-Holocene high sea stand observed in the Marshalls, Kiribati and Tuvalu groups (Athens 1995, Dye 1987). A raised reef platform suggests a necessarily higher sea level in order to accommodate the growth of the reef (Athens 1995); this in turn, has repercussions on the status of the present shoreline. With higher sea levels, the corresponding shoreline would have been somewhat more inland; a drop in sea level would initiate a lagoonward expansion of the island's shoreline, eventually forming the modern pattern.

Roughly between 3500 and 2000 B.P. (years before present), according to Athens (1995), sea levels were anywhere from one to two meters higher than today. Studies in the Central Pacific atoll groups have verified this higher sea level (Buddemeier, Smith and Kinzie 1975, Dye 1987, Athens 1995). Athens' (1995) own studies on the exposed Kosrae reef structures provide compelling evidence that Kosrae too experienced higher sea levels during this time period. The older and higher of the two formations he studied, the Sroanef formation, is dated between 1215 and 804 B.C., which corresponds with relict high sea stands observed in the Marshalls and the other regional atoll groups (Athens 1995). The second, slightly lower formation, Pukusruk Te formation, is dated between A.D. 1062 and 1362, which, according to Athens (1995), indicates that sea levels did not stabilize to modern levels until *after* this date (the Marshall Islands data also suggest as much; Dye 1987). The Pukusruk Te formation could be interpreted as an intermediary stage, marking a point of sea stand stabilization within an overall trend of decreasing sea levels that began with the formation of Sroanef.

Beyond the shores of Kosrae, there are no outlying islands, unlike the seas surrounding other high volcanic islands. But then, the submarine landscape in the immediate vicinity does not seem particularly conducive to the formation of thick basement structures of limestone which would in turn support such islands. No other isolated hot spots occur in the immediate vicinity of Kosrae, nor are there any zones of hot spots such as those associated with the basal structures of Tuvalu, Kiribati or the Marshall Islands (Nunn 1994).

## Climate and Hydrology

Kosrae enjoys a fairly benign climate that is uniformly hot and humid, with little intra-annual variation and few major storms. Overall, the climate is characterized by high rainfall, high temperatures and high humidity; it truly deserves the name 'tropical.' The 19th century explorers and navigators made particular note of the heat and humidity they experienced while on-island. Lesson, for example, commented on the excessively hot days, describing the heat as murderous and making their stay very uncomfortable (Ritter and Ritter 1982). Duperrey's comments focus on the permanently wet soil across the island and its affect of tempering the heat, making their days slightly more bearable (Ritter and Ritter 1982).

Rainfall too is abundant, and probably forms the second major climatic characteristic of Kosrae. On average, rainfall amounts hover around 500 cm in the footslopes and along the narrow coastal strand (Leluh, on the lee side, receives about 475 cm or 190 inches annually; Mwot, on the windward, receives roughly 650 cm or 260 inches annually), with the higher elevations receiving an estimated 750 cm annually (Cordy 1993). Elevation plays a major role in influencing rainfall amounts, and temperatures for that matter. Higher elevations convectively increase precipitation from passing rain clouds; and as if in direct correlation, they correspondingly promote cooler air circulation, so that higher altitudes display a greater variation between daytime and nighttime temperatures. There are no records for either rainfall or temperature variation in the higher elevations of the island; needless to say, while there is a greater chance you will be colder and wetter, temperatures are still well above freezing. The official, reported average annual temperatures for Kosrae are calculated from readings taken at weather stations placed throughout the modern, inhabited areas of the island, that is, on the lower elevations of the coastal strand and the adjoining footslopes. From these records, the average annual temperature for Kosrae is about 27° C (81° F), and varies roughly one degree from one month to the next. Within this region of the Pacific, the relatively constant temperature of the tropical waters acts as the principal determinant of temperature and humidity (Nunn 1994), ensuring that temperatures (and humidity and rainfall) do not swing wildly from one extreme to another.

Few major storms cross paths with Kosrae, in part because the storm track in this part of the Pacific generally forms to the west, between Kosrae and Chuuk. From a global perspective, such storms are generally absent in the equatorial zone between 5° N and 5° S latitude, where persistent high pressure prevents their development (Nunn 1994). When major storms do hit the island, they are considered unusual events and often become the core of time-reckoning oral histories, serving as reference points in historical narrative. Many of these major storms can be traced to global perturbations in weather patterns and the appearance of the El Nino-Southern Oscillation phenomenon (Nunn 1994). These events are associated with extreme weather conditions, which generally result in a disruption of normal rainfall and wind patterns, causing droughts in some areas and higher than average rainfall in others, increased temperatures, intensification and changes in storm patterns, and even shifts in ocean currents (which can have catastrophic effects on marine ecosystems).

The proximity of Kosrae to the inter-tropical convergence zone, where the dominant weather patterns of the northern and southern hemisphere meet, plays a major role in the overall character of Kosrae's weather patterns. Generally, there are only two 'seasons' on the island, a dry season and a wet season, each influenced by shifting wind patterns. January, for example, marks the onset of the dry season, as the wind pattern is dominated by the northeast tradewinds. Off-shore winds are more noticeable at this time, and although rainfall tends to decrease there are still significant accumulations; it is not really a 'dry' season per se, but one in which there is merely *less* rainfall. In July, the winds begin to gradually shift to the west, marking the onset of the wet season. As a transition month, July experiences unpredictable wind patterns, and as the winds change so do the ocean currents. To the locals, July is known as the 'fishless' month (personal communication, fishermen in Walung, July 2001), when neither the weather nor fish patterns can be predicted.

Kosrae has been called an island of wetlands, in part because it supports a large number of perennial water courses. Its geology might be regarded as one of the more important controls on the overall drainage pattern, influencing the course of drainage, the amount of downcutting a river experiences, the meanders and loops of stream branches, and the formation of a floodplain of semiswampland that feeds into the mangrove swamps surrounding the island. Needless to say, the island is well-watered, and not just from the amount of rain that falls annually. There are a number of permanent and intermittent rivers and streams that criss-cross the island; these provide a source of water for human transport, consumption, fishing, and even horticulture. In the journals of the 19th century visitors, their cross-island travel is described as following many rivers, streams, and even an occasional waterfall (Ritter and Ritter 1982). Given the thick proliferation of vines and other vegetation covering and even obscuring the ground surfaces, these waterways actually prove more efficient as a means of travel. Some of the rivers and streams are fed by springs, others simply channel rainwater downslope, and all ultimately drain into the mangroves, feeding this unique ecosystem with a flush of nutrients carried from the upslope regions of the island. The mouths of the main rivers (named above) form the principal bays and anchorages within the lagoon just beyond the mangroves, bringing with them a rush of freshwater to commingle with saltwater and create brackish pools. There are no lakes on the island, but the narrow coastal plain is replete with freshwater swamps.

**Flora and Fauna**

The biotic elements in the Kosrae environment are quite numerous. Unfortunately, general studies are not available and no systematic collections have been made. As in tropical areas elsewhere, the amount of living material is substantial and is represented by a variety of species. A large portion of the flora, for example, is used as food, raw material, firewood, medicine, ornaments, ceremonial purposes, and perhaps other uses no longer recognized today. The fauna too are represented by a diversity of forms. Several species are considered principal sources of food (especially from the marine ecosystems), while others are highly prized for certain products, such as feathers or teeth. In the following discussion, species identifications are presented with great trepidation given the absence of specific studies; neither accuracy nor completeness should be expected. There are, for example, what appears to be several distinct species of breadfruit, but without an accurate scientifically generated species list, it would be highly misleading to make a specific identification *as if* a determination had actually been made.

Basically, Kosrae is richly endowed with a variety of plants, in part because of the amount of relief in its topography, as well as its high humidity, rainfall and

Figure 3. A sampling of various plant domesticates and plants of use: a. coconut; b. Bird's Foot fern, used medicinally; c. breadfruit, the staple plant in Kosraean subsistence; d. *ka'a*, a Polynesian almond used to make canoes; e. *noni*, an Indian mulberry, used medicinally.

temperature, all of which work in concert to form something like a greenhouse that promotes impressive plant growth and fluorescence. There are, for example, a number of trees that yield suitable building materials for items such as posts and thatching. Others are large enough and long enough for the manufacture of canoes. While the canoe outrigger, attachments, even the poles and oars used to propel the canoe are manufactured from still other trees and woody plants found throughout a diverse number of ecosystems across the island. There are also a number of other plants that are used as a source of fiber used in weaving baskets, nets and other implements, including the manufacture of the finely patterned *tol* cloth for which Kosrae is known. Flowers and seeds used as decorations, medicines, even fish poisons are drawn from the floral kingdom of the island. Many of the more useful plants are encouraged to grow near occupations today, but they were also used in traditional times with the result that earlier plantings have now spread throughout the grounds of archaeological sites (Figure 3).

Passage through any of the forested areas on-island reinforces a commonly accepted perspective that these tropical forests are in large part secondary. They are no longer pristine, but the result of extensive ancient cultivation, selective use, and the encouragement of growth and expansion of certain economic species over others. This former disturbance has promoted an environment dominated by invasive species, as opposed to incipient ones. Certainly the plants commonly associated with traditional, archaeological sites were given this initial advantage; during the development of secondary forests, they were protected and encouraged to expand owing to the cultural preferences for their specific qualities.

A vast range of domesticated food plants are grown throughout the island, including a number that were introduced by the founding population, as well as subsequent waves of prehistoric, traditional and even historical settlers. Like many other Micronesian islands, Kosrae supported a wide range of domesticated plant species, many of which spilled over from established gardens gone wild and spread throughout the island. The early populations were also actively managing extensive agroforestry zones, cultivating and selectively encouraging the growth and spread of plants important in subsistence, as well as other economic activities. A few of the more important plants include taro, yams, bananas, breadfruit, tapioca, sugarcane, papaya, and many medicinal plants. Breadfruit was one of the principal arboreal contributions to the diet as well as the culture. According to Lesson, breadfruit furnished the principal base of existence; it was observed everywhere, in the mountains as well as in established crops, and was so common that the fruit littered the ground (Ritter and Ritter 1982). Coconut, citrus and pandanus also grow throughout the island and play a major role in local subsistence, but their presence as either native or introduced species remains a controversial subject (Figure 3a).

Continuing with the faunal component of the biota, the island is inhabited seasonally by a number of long ranging sea birds, which occupy nesting sites a short time each year. A number of terrestrial birds are also present on-island, some of which have entered the traditional cultural system as food or feathers, others because their eerie solitary cries play a role in oral histories and traditional beliefs. Of the limited range of native terrestrial fauna, the only endemic mammal, the fruit bat, served as both a source of food and legend; other members of the terrestrial population include various amphibians, reptiles and insects. None of the latter appears to have been a source of food, at least for the human population. Species counts in off-shore waters, however, easily surpassed the number of terrestrial species. Both the shallow and deep off-shore waters supported a wealth of marine species within and outside the reef; shellfish, crustaceans, marine invertebrates, turtles, marine mammals, reef fish, flying fish, and pelagic fish appear at various times of the year in the waters surrounding Kosrae. The products of this ecosystem provide the majority of sustenance, in both traditional times and today. Archaeological records (Athens 1995, Cordy 1993, Ritter and Ritter 1982, Welch et al. 1990) indicate that traditional Kosraean subsistence appears to have been based predominately on marine organisms, such as shellfish and a wide range of reef and off-shore fish (Figure 4). Turtles too played a major role in the cultural system, as they provided eggs, meat, and carapace, but they also came to represent high status; only chiefs and other high status members of society could eat turtle or don the ornaments made from their remains.

Spiders, arthropods, and other insects and wee beasties are another category of fauna for which a full species list does not exist, yet no description of a tropical environment would be complete without them. The most frequently felt insects are mosquitoes and sand fleas. The former are denizens of wet, marshy areas, and as Kosrae has been described as an island of wetlands, the occurrence of these implacable nuisances is ubiquitous. Sand fleas too, make their presence felt, often with bites that far exceed the annoyances of any mosquito. These creatures have been described as having a bite equivalent to the hard pointed beak of a bird being driven deep into your skin; as such, they have been described as 'small chickens in the sand' (personal communication, residents of Walung, July 2001). Some of the more beautiful insects are the many species of butterflies found in shady areas of the forest, with their brilliant colors and multiple hues calling attention to their presence. On occasion, they land on your hand or arm and lap up the moisture and salt that accumulates in small beads of sweat. Termites too are endemic; their persistence is one of the reasons why tropical houses are so perishable. One of the more frightening arthropods is the scorpion, although bees and wasps probably sting more frequently than they do.

Faunal species introduced to the island by the waves of human populations include rats, an ubiquitous stow-away in virtually all voyaging canoes, dogs, and possibly monitor lizards (records of the 19th century visitors make note of a giant lizard on-island; Ritter and Ritter 1982). According to Athens (1995), there is no evidence for prehistoric era pigs in archaeological contexts, which fits well within a general pattern of absence throughout

Figure 4. Pigs and reef fish, two common faunal elements in the subsistence regimen of traditional Kosrae.

Micronesia[1]. Although, there are historical accounts related to the introduction of the pig on Kosrae (Ritter and Ritter 1982). Today, pigs play a major role in ceremonial exchanges and feasts, and the hunt for wild pigs in the forests that cover the island provide recreation for only the most skilled of hunters (Figure 4).

All the fauna mentioned above (and this by no means constitutes a full list), whether endemic or introduced, serve as a source of food, beauty, raw materials, nuisances, or even disease and illness for the human population. They also present another source of threat, especially to economic resources, in part because they produce or play host to the genesis of worms and other destructive larvae. Pests include rats, birds, various insects, ants, rampaging wild pigs, even domesticated pigs that root up gardens and archaeological sites. The class of pests can also be expanded to include fungi, molds, bacteria, viruses, and other microbes.

At the very least, this short review of the island's floral and faunal populations suggests the Kosraeans cohabited with a farrago of many living companions. Some were of their own choosing, most were not.

**Walung and Safonfok**

In addition to the general comments presented above, our own observations over two seasons of fieldwork provide few additional details. The site of Safonfok is located on the southwest coast of the island, in the region referred to as Walung. This area consists of a narrow coastal strand distributed between an active beach that serves as interface with the lagoon, and a back-beach deposit of stabilized sands supporting a dense jungle of strand-adapted vegetation; thick mangroves in all those areas

where fresh water is flushed and filtered from the mountains into the lagoon, along river channels and river mouths; steep mountain slopes that ascend into the island's interior; and several permanent and intermittent stream and river drainages. Today, Walung is considered one of the richest fisheries on the island, but this is possibly because it is also the last area to have a road connecting it to the rest of the island (this is changing, however, as construction was underway in the summer of 2001 to extend the circumferential road into Walung from the south).

Walung encompasses a number of ecozones, each representing in microcosm the full array of diversity found across the rest of the island (Figure 5). The mountain slopes are covered in a thick, matted jungle vegetation; the mangroves are extensive and support a wide range of terrestrial and aquatic flora and fauna; the coastal strand supports a vegetation community suitable to its sandy soils, although somewhat sparser than that found in the jungles or mangroves. Pigeons are hunted in the jungles of Walung today, as are wild boar. Herons roost in the trees along the shoreline, and other marine and terrestrial birds dart from one tree to the next in search of insects, nectar and nesting areas. Seagrass meadows dominate much of the shallows in the lagoon, coexisting with a wide range of corals. Here, a variety of shellfish, crustaceans, marine invertebrates, and a wide diversity of fish can be found, some trying to avoid capture by darting between corals or hiding in the meadows. Beyond the reef, the off-shore waters are teaming with all variety of pelagic fish; schools of tuna, dolphin, flying fish, and sharks forage these waters.

Safonfok itself is located on a back-beach deposit, on a narrow finger of the coastal strand separated from the rest of the island by a wide mangrove channel. Safonfok lies just inland from the active beach, well ensconced in the atoll-strand vegetation community that dominates this environment. Soils in this area are described as

---

[1] Recent work by Intoh (1986, 1996) on Fais is slowly changing this perception. She has identified the whole set of Austronesian domesticated animals—dog, pig and chicken—in early deposits on this Micronesian low island.

Ngedubus loamy sand (a deep, excessively drained sandy soil common to coastal strands on the island; USDA 1983), one of several different kinds of soils found on the island. Most of the soils on Kosrae are derived from basic igneous rock, mainly basalt, andesite, and trachyte lava flows and dikes; other soil types are formed in organic deposits; and still other soils, like Ngedubus, formed in coral sands (USDA 1983).

Figure 5. Footbridge across the mouth of the mangrove in Walung (at low tide).

Safonfok rests at an elevation of about 8 meters above mean sea level, which would place it above even the highest sea stands of the past, as evidenced in the raised reef samples discussed above. Coconuts, breadfruit, pandanus, papaya, banyon, hibiscus, a variety of medicinal plants, and plants used for ornaments and firewood appear within and immediately outside the limits of the site. Herons, fruit doves, pigeons, pigs, land crabs, monitor lizards, and insects were noted in the site area. The site itself is known locally as a rich environment for land crabs, and has been mined for these critters during the Mission era of the late 19th and the first part of the 20th centuries. Their burrows form an intricate, interconnected web of transects that criss-cross the sandy soil of the area, undermining wall foundations and making foot travel perilous. Pigs too have delivered another kind of damage to the site; their rooting through the soil and decaying tree trunks has mixed sediments, especially in the lagoonward portion of the site, and dislodged wall components.

With the exception of the discussion on geology, information on the natural environment of Walung and Safonfok is almost entirely confined to contemporary circumstances. But it can also provide a basis for estimating the environment and range of natural materials available to the prehistoric, traditional era occupants of the site. Our initial working assumptions for fieldwork were that site occupants made wide use of the aquatic resources, finding this environment a rich source of sustenance and materials for tools, ornaments, and construction, as well as a key component in their transportation system; that the land-based biota provided a wide array of materials for canoes, decoration, house construction, firewood, medicines, food, and other economic necessities; that their technological systems were well adapted toward the use of locally available materials such as shell, coral, stone, and wood. How site occupants managed to modify and tame this environment to suit their basic life needs, as well as to fulfill more complex goals related to growing political, social and economic organization, is another dimension of a larger investigation focused on examining the full range of interrelated components that is Safonfok.

## Cultural Context

With the arrival of the first human settlers, Walung and the rest of the island began to change in more ways than just the physical environment. It became a place imbued with magical and mystical qualities. This part of the island, the southwestern region, would also play a key role in the rise of influential political leaders in the history of Kosrae. It was the place with long ties to the past, the 'land of the ancestors,' where families could trace their roots to the men and women who first set foot on the island. But, how much has been recorded, compiled or even remembered about this first settlement and the traditions these men and women brought with them? How much is recorded in myth, legend, oral history, historical observations, and ethnography? How often were these various histories recounted and passed on from one generation to the next? And, how much has slipped quietly away from the collective consciousness with little notice, all in an effort to conform to an imported religion, a new social organization, an alien world beyond the shores of the island, and all spurred on through the agency of missionaries and the establishment of foreign colonies?

Precious little information exists in sufficient detail to address any of these questions. Current reconstructions of the island's social and political history point to a domination by the eastern center of Leluh over the whole island at the time European explorers arrived. The rise and fall of Walung in Kosrae history, from initial settlement to its final struggle for control within the trans-island power structure is a story that remains to be told. How Leluh achieved its place in Kosraean history, and Walung lost its place within the power structure, is the stuff of archaeology. But here the picture becomes somewhat blurred. The nature of the occupation in Walung and across the island is ambiguous, although evidence for at least a persistence of occupation and a human presence is compelling. And what of Safonfok? Little can be said, so far. This is a site seemingly removed from historical events or at least those events that have been recorded by scholars and archaeologists documenting traditional, pre-Contact Kosrae.

The succeeding pages will attempt to create a cultural framework and establish a context for understanding the results of fieldwork, much the same way the previous section described the environmental setting of Walung, and more specifically Safonfok. This section begins with an account of Walung and its role in myth, legend and oral history, and attempts to establish a portrait of the late prehistoric/Contact era occupation of the area and the island. It is followed by a section on previous archaeological research, which lays the foundation for hypothetical reconstructions of the past from a time outside oral history. For our purposes, it is useful to begin with the known and work our way into the unknown, recognizing that the paths from past to present are many, marked by events written in abbreviated fashion through the scattered evidence of tangible material remains. It is up to us to interpret the path or paths represented by those remains, knowing full well that no matter which route of interpretation is taken, it must end in the present, it must at a minimum create a viable transition into the events and circumstances observed at Contact.

**Legendary Visions**

When the first waves of early settlers arrived, they brought with them many material items that were necessary for their survival. Among those 'purposeful introductions' were basic subsistence plants such as taro, yams, breadfruit, bananas, tapioca, papaya, sugar cane, medicinal plants, and perhaps even coconuts and pandanus. But they also carried with them those intangible elements of their ancestral traditions that were probably even more important to their survival in a hostile, unknown land: knowledge of the development and manufacture of utilitarian items, ornaments and talismans; architectural plans; models for settlement systems, as well as the organizational ability to rally, direct and manage a growing population; and, rudimentary skills necessary for the strategic execution and improvisation of landscape modification, and the exploitation of both terrestrial and marine resources. This ancestral population also carried with them the vestiges of their ancestors, numerous non-material elements that were of importance to their psychological well-being and by which they could retain strong ties to their past. It is this intangible culture, such as a pantheon

of local gods and ancestral spirits, as well as valuable information on traditions, practices, beliefs, place names, and historical events, that is the substance of legendary narratives, chants, songs, and dances, all of which are part of that anthropological realm of expressive arts. Such narratives and other creative acts were passed down through the generations, and were intended to teach as well as entertain, to instill a sense of historical continuity, and to perpetuate a common social and political identity and heritage in the listeners, observers and participants.

Few traditional narratives remain intact, as Sarfert (1919, 1920) noted during his stay on the island as a member of the German Sudsee Expedition in 1910. The youngest generation, he lamented, do not know their own past and culture (Sarfert 1919). This was the same observation made in 1880 by Finsch of the Boston Mission, just 30 years prior to Sarfert's arrival. What remained in the minds of the island inhabitants were mere fragments of a formerly rich history filled with deities that reigned supreme over some realm or other of nature, as well as deified ancestors, impish spirits, hero stories, and ambiguous histories embedded within clan names. Other stories vaguely relay potentially significant information about those places that harbor the souls of the dead, as well as love magic and the magic used in important undertakings like the construction of a canoe or fishing, proper and improper behavior, the level of respect accorded specific title-holders, and even fanciful fables used to entertain children in the dark of night.

With little continuity in the surviving body of oral histories, the mythic and historic eras blend almost imperceptibly. From whence, for example, did the first settlers come? No one history, or even a combination of various historical fragments points to any one particular place or direction. There are, for instance, connections to Yap (especially with respect to traditional deities), several islands in the Central Pacific including the Marshall Islands, Pingelap (once considered very close to Kosrae, but pushed away by the thoughtless actions of a God), Ngatik (Sapwuahfik), Pohnpei and Chuuk, the Mortlock group, Banaba, Tuvalu and Kiribati, as well as the Polynesian island of Tonga (home of the 'southern tradition' and the oldest lineage on the island). Do any of these places represent a point of origin for the people of Kosrae? We can merely speculate at this point, using as our foundation for a reasonable, best-guess scenario material culture remains, linguistic similarities and differences, oral histories from these various islands, and even botanical remains.

At the very least, this recurring list of islands in song and saga demonstrates the expansive geographical coverage of the ancient Kosraeans. Their motives for these sundry voyages were the same as those throughout the Pacific: family ties, military expeditions, religious dependence, and trading networks (Sarfert 1919). Kosrae, for instance, was the trading center for turmeric, or 'red dye root,' along with mats, woven belts and breadfruit, while red shell beads and drums could be obtained from the Marshalls, pearl shell fishhooks and currency came from the islands to the west, and sennit came from various islands throughout the region (except for Kosrae, which had a scarcity of coconut palms, but which used an inordinately large amount of sennit; Sarfert 1919). There are also hero stories and legendary accounts that relay feats of adventure, victory and cultural exchanges between Kosrae and the islands of Micronesia. There is, for example, one great national myth glorifying a successful military expedition against Pohnpei, and in another example, a well-known and continuously recounted story about the travels of Sinlaka, the breadfruit goddess, between Yap and Kosrae (Sarfert 1919).

In the war against Pohnpei, Sarfert (1919) relates two versions of this event, although he says in a footnote that he heard a number of versions during his stay on the island (which is in keeping with the traditions of oral history, where no one 'correct' account of a story exists). The following is the more detailed of the two versions recorded by Sarfert; it is entitled *Nepartak*, after the name of the hero. Other versions of this story describe the number of warriors as 333, no more and no less; still others refer to the hero by the name of Selbas (as in this version) rather than Nepartak; while other versions incorporate the actions of the Thunder God within the unfolding events of the conflict. Pohnpei too has its own versions of this same story, only the hero bears the name of Isokelekel (Bernart 1977, Ashby 1989).

> Once upon a time in Ponape, two kings fought against each other, the Nainmariki of Kitty and Salikfas of Lot in Metalanim. King Lot was very mighty and had many people; Nainmariki, however, felt himself too weak. Therefore he pulled back and thought about who would be strong enough to be able to help him. In a circle on the ground, he made symbols that were each supposed to signify one island group, the Marshall Islands, the Gilbert Islands, Kosrae, Pingelap, Mokil, and other islands. Then he took an entire coconut, carved a groove into it, which signified his person, and placed it inside the circle of symbols on the ground; he started it spinning with a swing. The notch remained near the sign for Kosrae. Then he sent two men to Kosrae with the coconut. When they got there, they kept out of sight, but rather, threw the coconut onto the outer beach of Lolo at the place called Inop, and sailed back. An old Kosraean woman, Nisalsai by name, just then came back from fishing, and felt hungry. Then she found the old coconut, which was already sprouting. She picked it up, broke it open, and ate it. In spite of the fact that the woman was too old to bear children, she

became pregnant by the coconut, and bore a son, whom she named Selbas.

One day, the child played at the place called Kenuen in Lolo with a half a coconut shell, which he repeatedly dropped on a rock. Each time the coconut shell shot into the air, which delighted the child. He loudly shouted for joy. Then Sebas, an old man, came down the path; he was a noble, and a relative of the king's mother. When he saw the met-sisik child playing and heard him loudly shouting for joy, he took a stick and beat him enough to have killed him. The child, however, ran away to the place called Jutak, where he again played as before on a black rock. But Sebas followed him and beat him again. Then the boy raced to Matannenea on Ualang and ran along the east coast to the south coast, to the district of Likinlolam. There Selbas lived until he became a man. Every day he drank the bitter medicine made of Kamuok, so that he would become strong. He was also like a spirit. If one went from one house, where they had just seen him and spoken with him, and into another house, he was also present there.

Once upon a time, the king declared a war against Ponape to conquer it. All the men built a single large canoe, in which there was room for several hundred people. They boarded in the district of Jola on Ualang; everyone sat down on the platform in the middle. Then Sebas said, "Bring Selbas along!" They went to Likinlolam to fetch him. In the one house, they asked, "Where is Selbas?" Selbas, who was himself being addressed, answered, "In the next house." They went there. In the meantime, Selbas was already there, and when asked, answered in the same manner. So it went. Finally the searchers realized that it was always the same man whom they met in the houses and who answered them, and they saw from this that it was Selbas himself. They brought him to Jola. Then the people asked, "What, that's Selbas? We thought he was a strong man; that is a boy!" Selbas did not reply. They now instructed him to keep bailing out the bilges. Selbas submitted. The canoe set sail for Ponape. Selbas always bailed water, while the others sat on the platform. Two days later, he asked the others, "Where's land? Have you sighted it?" They answered, "No we still don't see anything." Selbas again asked, "Don't you see any birds?" They answered him, "Yes, just now a suk (frigate bird) is flying above the canoe." Then Selbas looked up, leaped out of the hold and into the air, and grabbed the bird with his hand. He gave the body to the others, but the wings he kept for himself. Then some said, "The boy is no human, he's a spirit." The others, however, mocked, "The boy! He is not at all strong and not smart, and where does he come from? He doesn't even have a father!"

Finally the canoe arrived at <u>Kitty</u> in Ponape, and they went ashore. The king of <u>Kitty</u> saw the Kosraeans coming, and wanted at first to have his people attack them. But the queen said, "No, let them live, they can work for us, make spears, and wage war." Then the king thought, "Well, let them live." The Kosraeans, however, went into the bush, made spears for themselves, and then attacked the Ponapeans. Twice they attacked the king's residence, but both times they were repulsed.

<u>Selbas</u> was not permitted to fight, but rather, had to stay near the canoe. When he saw his people returning, he called to them, "You are cowardly! Stay here near the canoe now. I will go alone and defeat the Ponapeans!" They mocked him out and shouted, "How are you singlehandedly going to defeat the Ponapeans, when all of us had to retreat from them? You're out of your mind!" <u>Selbas</u> answered, "Just wait, I'm going to fight them alone." He stuck the two frigate bird wings in his hair, one on each side, and went in front of the house of the king of <u>Kitty</u>, and sat down there. When the king spied the frail young man, he asked, "What do you want? Do you want to have a breadfruit?" <u>Selbas</u> replied, "No!" In the same manner, the king asked him about all the fruits. <u>Selbas</u> always simply replied, "No!" Finally the queen picked up a rock and asked, "Do you want to have some of this?" <u>Selbas</u> answered, "Yes!" Then the king shouted, "Wait, let me call my mightiest warrior!" He came; his name was <u>Bantentloin</u>. The king told him what he had asked the boy, and that he wanted to fight. Then <u>Bantentloin</u> called out, "What, I've fought off your entire people, and now here comes this boy to fight with me?" He took a stone and threw it at <u>Selbas</u> and called, "Konam?" as he did so, <u>Selbas</u> replied, "<u>Beti!</u>" and caught it in midair with the back of his hand, his arm outstretched. He drew his arm back, so that the rock would roll forward back down his arm, and grabbed it with his hand. While doing so, he calmly remained seated on the ground, and placed the rock under his right buttock, so that he sat on it. <u>Bantentloin</u> grabbed a second rock and threw it at <u>Selbas</u>. He caught it on the fly in the same manner as previously with his left hand, and placed it under his left buttock. So the battle went, until <u>Selbas</u> was finally sitting on a big pile of rocks. When <u>Bantentloin</u> no

longer had any stones, he called to <u>Selbas</u>, "Now you throw!" <u>Selbas</u> remained sitting, took a rock from the pile on which he sat, threw it and called, "Konam!" <u>Banentloin</u> replied, "Beti," but could not catch the stone in midair with his hand. Rather, it tore off his left arm. The next rock ripped off his right arm, and the third, his thorax, so that he died. Finally all the Ponapeans came to fight against <u>Selbas</u>, but he slew them all with his stone throwing. The pile of stones that <u>Selbas</u> had built up from the shots of his opponent is still present to this day in Ponape.

When <u>Selbas</u> had destroyed all the people of Ponape, he took a young man and a girl from Kosrae, who were to stay behind in Ponape, and said to the rest of his countrymen, "You sail back to Kosrae, I'm staying here." The Kosraeans sailed home; <u>Selbas</u>, however, went out onto the reef near the coast and that big pile of rocks, and there he turned himself into a large block of stone, which lies there to this day.

The king of <u>Kitty</u> is familiar with the pile of rocks and this large rock; and all Ponape knows of the great war, but does not like to speak of it. The new population of Ponape descends from the Kosraean couple who were left behind. After his victory, <u>Selbas</u> received the nickname <u>Nepartak</u>. [Sarfert 1919]

Within the traditional religion on Kosrae, the pantheon of natural or supreme deities and ancestral spirits provided guidance for nearly every aspect of daily life and annual ritual, from canoe building to the harvesting of breadfruit to the routines of weaving and gardening. Many of the deities, according to the oral traditions, made their home on Yap. One deity in particular occupied a significant place in the traditional religion: Sinlaka, the goddess of breadfruit, who could do many things including conger typhoons, famines, droughts, and when a specific type of punishment was needed, introduce disease (thought to be influenza). She had the power of life and death over humans, according to Sarfert (1919), as she controlled the ripening of breadfruit and could influence the forces of nature. She is credited with at least three typhoons that 'destroyed the island,' causing famines and great hardships; during one, *paka los*, a giant wave engulfed Kosrae and destroyed everything (Sarfert 1919). The power of Sinlaka over the Kosraeans was so strong that Reverend Snow found himself competing against her in his mission to christianize the island. It is said, according to local histories, that Sinlaka, upon seeing the future of her people and the dawning of a new religion, left Kosrae forever and fled to Yap.

Sinlaka had two places of worship on the island: a house at the foot of Tafonkol in a place called Fal in Fenkol, and another house in the district of Funfukul in Uia, or Wiya (Sarfert 1919). Both houses were considered *tapu*; they were only repaired and rebuilt when a new king (or paramount chief) ascended to the throne. Each of the houses belonged to a one of the two priestly societies that ministered to the goddess and served as mediaries between the people of Kosrae and Sinlaka. They were responsible for the timing and performance of the various rituals and ceremonies dedicated to her. And, upon the ascension of a new king, the priestly societies would erect a new house for the goddess and from there plan and direct the procession to take place in advance of the coronation, prepare a feast for the day of the coronation, instruct their followers in stick fighting, and provide offerings to the goddess over *kava* (or *seka*). By the time Sarfert arrived on-island, the obligations of the priestly societies were virtually unknown, except one in particular, the procession and rituals involved with the breadfruit harvest:

> The various varieties of breadfruit do not yield a uniformly abundant harvest year after year. They are supposed to bear very heavily every three years. When this large harvest was imminent, Sinlaka came, as the natives put it. According to the story of an old man in Uia, the following arrangements were made in Uia. The priests built a new house and in it prepared a tanes (breadfruit picker). Then they went to a breadfruit tree and seated themselves underneath it, while one of the priests climbed the tree and pulled off breadfruit, that is, only for the various titular chiefs in Lolo; as he did so, with each fruit he loudly cried, "For the king! For Kanko!" etc. They took the fruit into the goddess' house and prepared furo out of it. Only then could the population of Uia, Sialat, Matante, and Tafonsak, the districts on the northern coast of Ualang, also harvest breadfruit and prepare furo. It took about fourteen days before this was ready. During this period, the priests stayed in the house of the goddess and drank kava morning and evening, during which the chief priest Kaijen recited a prayer. The people of the aforementioned districts had to bring a portion of the prepared furo to the priests, who then staged a big feast. For this, the priests' wives went fishing out on the reef with masa nets; they went to a certain large rock, which they moved. Beforehand the priest Losa had placed four sugarcane leaves, which had been crushed in his hand, underneath this rock to serve as fish food. This fishing expedition was a formality. Without catching any fish, the women went home and ate the feast consisting of furo. [Sarfert 1919]

Sarfert records one other story about Sinlaka, taken from the notes of a local teacher in Malem. The notes were written for use in school and date to 1896. The author, however, died several years prior to the arrival of Sarfert and the Hamburg Expedition:

> Two men from Uia, Sauuia and Lopanpital by name, did not bother with her service, and went fishing. During fishing, they drifted away to Yap in their canoe. Sinlaka was angry that the two had not attended to her worship. When the two arrived in Yap, they did not know the name of the island. Only later did they learn that the island belonged to Sinlaka. When they walked around the island, they saw a woman sitting in a house who looked like Kaien's wife in Uia. They entered the house, and the woman asked them, "Who are you, are you humans or spirits?" She further remarked that no one came to the island, no rat, no fly, no human, nothing. Then she asked, "Which island is your home?" The two answered, "We come from Uia!" The woman continued, and asked them how they got there. The one answered that they had gone fishing and drifted off. The woman asked, "What do the people in Uia do?" The men answered, "The people of Uia were preparing a feast for Sinlaka on the day on which we went fishing." The woman asked, "Which feast?" They answered, "Koasok-ipenie." The woman asked, "To whom does koasok-ipenie belong?" They answered, "It belongs to Kasoa Sinlaka!" Then Sinlaka said to them, "I am Sinlaka! I do not want you to go fishing before my service is over!"

> When the men were there a while, Sinlaka commanded them to fetch some ika wood and to set up a small ground oven. They did so, and erected a small hum. Sinlaka commanded them to fill two coconut shells with water, one with fresh water, the other with saltwater. They placed the shells in the ground oven and covered them up. Then she commanded them to plait many baskets. The two men looked at her and laughed. They made as many baskets as they could. Then the goddess commanded them to remove all the leaves from the ground oven. Then they uncovered the ground oven, it was stuffed full of food: breadfruit, taro, bananas, yams, furo, fish, and many other things—totally full. Sinlaka ordered them to pack everything into the baskets. Then she invited the men to eat. But they could not eat everything. It was too much. One said to the other, "I would be happy if my children had some of that." Sinlaka did not look up at all, but rather had her eyes lowered and did some work. But she knew everything that they said. She asked them what they were talking about, but the two did not answer. She asked them

again. Then they answered, "We would be happy of our children had some of this fruit to eat." <u>Sinlaka</u> asked them to look into the air. They did so. After a while, the goddess requested that they look back down again. When they did so, nothing more was there.

Now <u>Sinlaka</u> showed them her entire locality. Many things were in her locality. A variety of breadfruit, <u>ek un lal</u>, was <u>Sinlaka's</u> favorite. When they had seen the locality, the goddess instructed the men to go to the beach and count the waves. When they counted the eighth wave, <u>Sinlaka</u> told them to close their eyes. They did so. After a while, when they opened their eyes, they saw their own village of <u>Uia</u> around them. They were in <u>Uia</u>. <u>Sinlaka</u> had previously told then to deliver a message to the people in <u>Uia</u>; they were to hold their worship service from then on. After they returned to <u>Uia</u>, the two men did not live for very long, but rather, soon died. The inhabitants of <u>Uia</u> and <u>Sialat</u> venerated <u>Sinlaka</u> for evermore. [Sarfert 1919]

The ancient religious practices and beliefs on Kosrae were nearly forgotten by the time Sarfert arrived. Few could not describe any of the rituals, the role of *seka* in these rituals, or for that matter the names or natures of the deities that had played such a decisive role in the lives of their forebears. Mere vestiges of these rites have survived, but they are so fragmentary as to remain enigmatic. According to Sarfert (1919), the old natives whom he encountered can remember enough to relate that the man of the house said a prayer addressing the deities in a murmuring voice before drinking *seka*. No one knew, he continued, which deity was referred to or which prayer was spoken (Sarfert 1919). Like so much of the history of Kosrae before the arrival of Europeans, much has been lost or abandoned, little has remained intact. Today, only fragments of memories have surreptitiously survived the condemnations, protests, restrictions, and prohibitions of the early Missionaries and their zealous program of conversion.

## Contact

By the time Europeans arrived in the first decades of the 19$^{th}$ century, the Kosraeans were already island-bound. Long-distance open ocean voyaging was a memory, active ties to overseas relatives and trading partners had long since been severed, and connections to the other islands in the region were relegated to accidental drift voyages and incidental landings from other places. With the first landings of the Europeans, the decline of traditional Kosraean culture accelerated. Hereditary succession to the throne was abandoned; the dual political structure based on a secular and religious authority vanished; the ancient system of land tenure was rapidly being abandoned as chiefs lost their absolute sovereignty and landed property became purely personal property; Leluh was losing its place of power and authority, displaced by the growing economic role of the main island within the new world order of colonial expansionism; and the already declining population was teetering precipitously close to extinction.

Sarfert notes that within a half century after Contact, the deep rooted indigenous culture of Kosrae was altered beyond recognition (Sarfert 1919). Ornamentation and tattooing disappeared; the old arts of weaving and manufacturing (weapons, tools and ornaments) were diminishing; fishing was confined to the reef; the ancient house with its keel-shaped roof, the coastal canoe and the ocean-going canoe either no longer existed or had undergone such significant changes that they were no longer recognizable. Sarfert (1919) noted that artistic undertakings were confined to the ornamentation of hatbands and stitched pouches made from pandanus. The ancient religion, he continued, had been stamped out, along with the other traditions such as dances, songs, myths, and games; likewise, all forms of tribute were abolished and age-old rituals were further weakened with prohibitions placed on all alcoholic beverages, especially the use of *seka,* and tobacco. Even the nature of traditional dress changed with the imposed adoption of the more modest (and highly impractical) dress of the missionaries (Sarfert 1919). New forms of housing, new settlement patterns, and new concepts of morality and law were forced onto this tractable population, along with a new social order, a new political order, and a new hybridization of western culture. The past was relegated to the memories of a few old men who happened to survive the ravages of the foreign onslaught of explorers, traders, buccaneers, proselytizers, colonizers, and the diseases they brought with them.

But, we are getting ahead of ourselves. First, we must get the Europeans to Kosrae.

The first tentative recognition of Kosrae by the western world appeared on a map from 1526, on which the island is identified as San Barthelemeo de Loyola (Ritter and Ritter 1982). There is no record of landings at that time, simply a map notation of its existence. Three years later, it was again sighted and recorded in the 1529 ship's logs of Alvaro de Saavedra, who may have spied the island from a distance. The next historical sighting we have for Kosrae appears nearly 250 years later when in 1787 it was identified as Carao. By the first decades of the 19$^{th}$ century, the *Gem of the Pacific* would become an almost regular and routine entry in the logs of passing ships. It received a wide array of names, from Strong Island (1804), to Hope Island (1807), Teyoa (1817), Experiment Island, Armstrong Island, and Quollen (Sarfert 1919), but was always recorded in roughly the same position.

The first landfalls by an outside vessel were the scientific expeditions of the *Coquille* in 1824, captained by Louis Isidore Duperrey, and the *Senyavin* in 1827/28, captained by Fyedor Lutke. Both referred to the island variously as

Ualar, Oualan, and Walan (Sarfert 1919, Ritter and Ritter 1982), names they obtained directly from the islanders. Both the Duperrey and Lutke expeditions left important in-depth accounts of their stays, recording both the natural and cultural environments. The name Kusaie would not appear in writing until 1880, when Finsch of the Boston Missionary Society wrote extensively about the island and its culture (Sarfert 1919). With the arrival of the French and Russian scientific expeditions, the floodgates were opened. The 1830s and 1840s saw a host of whalers, traders, castaways, beach combers, and deserters of all sorts arrive, take their rest and replenish supplies for their continued activities in this part of the Pacific. Even the infamous outlaw Bully Hayes took refuge on the island. By 1852, Reverend Snow and his entourage of Missionaries also made their way to the island, where they directed their Christian mission philosophy initially toward curbing the licentious behavior of the unruly western interlopers. Then, they turned their attention to the islanders themselves. Changes in traditional cultural practices were by then already underway. The Missionary societies, however, would simply complete the transformation (Figure 6).

Records of the earliest contact with the islanders are full of high praise. The people are described as peaceable like no other on the face of the earth, as well as good tempered, modest, honest, and hospitable to a fault (Sarfert 1919). They were organized into four distinct social strata, with the highest chief, the paramount, at the head of this organizational structure. The paramount served as both secular and sacred head of Kosraean society, and held title to all land (Athens 1995). The paramount, Cordy (1985) notes, appointed the highest priests to their positions and presided over religious ceremonies. Under the paramount, there were ten regional high chiefs, who were obliged to live in Leluh; it is here, under the watchful eye of the paramount, that they maneuvered for position and ranking, and consolidated power and alliances. Each high chief served as steward over several parcels of land, referred to as *facl*, each of which extended from the reef to the mountainous interior of the island (Cordy 1993, Athens 1995, Sarfert 1919). There were 50 such *facl* on the island (Sarfert 1919). Below the high chiefs were several lower chiefs, who oversaw the *facl* of their respective chiefs and in their turn resided on the land for which they were responsible. The lowest strata in Kosraean society consisted of the commoners, who may or may not have been entitled to smaller land parcels, but certainly held rights to various resources.

At Contact, Leluh was the administrative center of the island. It was the home of the paramount and the high chiefs, and it was the location foreign visitors and dignitaries were escorted for an audience with the 'king' (Ritter and Ritter 1982). To the populace at large, Leluh was the symbol of power, authority, influence, and island unification; all roads led to Leluh. According to Cordy

(1985, 1993), life on Leluh at Contact was infused with pomp and ceremony, with the architectural grandeur of this city-sized site reinforcing its position in Kosraean social order:

> The ruler and the high chiefs lived on Leluh along with commoners and servants. These servants (commoners) evidently performed fairly specialized tasks, such as infant care or food preparation. Leluh served as the political and sacred center of the Kosraean society. It covered about 40 ha and held 1200 to 1700 people. Leluh consisted of about 100 walled compounds (dwellings, two royal burial compounds, and 17 sacred compounds) connected by sea piers, an internal canal system, and a paved network of streets. The dwelling compounds of the four social strata differed greatly. The ruler's and high chiefs' dwelling compounds were clustered in central Leluh and had massive basalt walls as high as 6 m. Within were multiple houses, with a large feast-house near the main entrance. Here the ruler entertained his visitors and retinue. Earthen ovens were located near this feast house, and numerous food-pounding and *seka* (*Piper methysticum*)-pounding stones were present within the house. Behind the feast-house, a fence separated the private portion of the compound, comprised of several smaller houses—one for infants, one for servants, others for the wives of the ruler or lord, and one for the lord himself. The cemetery for the household was also usually located here... ([though the ruler was buried] in a special royal burial compound). In contrast, commoners' compounds had no walls or very small walls, no feast-house, no servants, and only one to three dwellings with a few food- and *seka*-pounding stones...On the main island, all households seem to have had one to three dwellings with small cemetery areas nearby. [Cordy 1985]

In the early historical accounts, Walung was the hinterland, the rural outback with a fairly small population that was farthest removed from Leluh as was physically possible. Further, these accounts describe the island interior as uninhabited. The earliest maps of the region show a sparsely populated island overall, with the majority of settlements lightly distributed along the coastal plain. The population census that accompany these maps note that seven men and six women were living within the *facl* of Leap, the only land parcel to encompass the general area of Safonfok (Ritter and Ritter 1982). Both Lutke and Lesson (the medical officer for Duperrey's expedition) indicate Leap on their respective maps of the island, but make no mention of Safonfok either in their records or on their maps. However, in Sarfert's (1919) geography of the island, Safonfok is

Figure 6. Traditional activities today, including a. net fishing (at dusk); b. boy poling sugar cane to market; c. making baskets (the one illustrated was a quickly fashioned utilitarian basket made from a coconut leaf; this one was used to carry and store our breadfruit); d. organ music for Congregationalist hymns introduced and translated by Missionaries.

mentioned as a small settlement within the west coast *facl* of Leap (every *facl* generally has more than one settlement within its expanse). It is described as a settlement consisting of a single dwelling, a cookhouse and a copra house (Sarfert 1919). Why the difference in information over a period of roughly 80 or 90 years? In part it may have to do with the manner in which information was obtained. Both Lutke and Lesson used a single informant, relying on his knowledge of the island as a whole. Sarfert, on the other hand, relied on the interpretive efforts of at least two gentlemen and the information they were able to draw from a number of local interviews conducted under the supervision of Sarfert himself. The difference in the nature and quality of information—the absence and then the appearance of Safonfok—may also have to do with the circumstances of history. In the intervening period, between the scientific expeditions of Duperrey and Lutke and the ethnographic investigation of Sarfert, missionaries arrived, converted the population to Congregationalism, established churches across the island, and built a mission in Mwot, just north of Safonfok and Leap. Our own oral history for the site (see below) makes mention of a Marshallese family that settled into the abandoned grounds of Safonfok in order to be closer to the Mwot Mission.

## Previous Archaeological Research

History has taken a heavy toll on Kosrae and its traditional culture, particularly the events of the last two centuries that accompanied the arrival of the western world. Kosraean culture has essentially remade itself to suit the demands of its most vocal oppressors who arrived under the guise of traders, colonizers and missionaries. In the process, the old ways have been pushed into obscurity, to slumber in a kind of oblivion. Every domain of traditional cultural practice has been dramatically reduced to isolated, discontinuous fragments where no one person seems to hold all the cues to understanding any one domain. Short threads of memory, some retained in surviving relics of oral history, still exist, alongside a landscape covered in architectural and material remnants that make up the archaeological record of the island. But what do they mean? Where do they fit into the larger history of the island? And, how do they relate to the historical sites and each odd smear of material culture? These are the questions of pure archaeology that feed into the overarching task of rescuing human history and interpreting a past from its material remains, with an occasional assist (if one is lucky) from a fragment or two of oral history.

The arrival of Sarfert and the German South Seas Expedition inaugurated the era of archaeological investigation on the island. Since then, the majority of the archaeological work has concentrated on Leluh and select areas within the coastal plain. Few, however, have focused on the island interior. The couple of brief archaeological surveys that did venture into the mountainous terrain of the island reported that it was indeed heavily occupied at one point, but when? And how was this occupation integrated into the political, economic and social affairs of the island? Our own brief traverse along a proposed road across the south end of the island during the 2001 field season demonstrated in no uncertain terms that there had been a heavy occupation in this area as well. The architectural remains we encountered were virtually continuous, with stone pavements, walled compounds, platforms, manicured and sculpted terrain with terraces cut into the sloped ground. All, however, had been so thoroughly covered in vines and other pioneering, jungled vegetation that often our first encounter with an architectural feature was felt with our feet. As we walked over the terrain, changes in the nature of the ground surface, such as a shift from volcanic soils and terrain to a concentration of cobbles and boulders, would bring us into direct contact with an archaeological site.

Archaeological work on Kosrae can be divided into two eras, the first covering the visit of the German South Seas Expedition, *the Early Years*, and the second, a more robust period of investigation under the auspices of the Trust Territory administration, *TT and CRM*. With each archaeological project, a little more of Kosrae's veiled past becomes visible. It is still fragmented, but at least a rough outline of sorts can be fashioned. Occupation on the island, for instance, appears at least 2,000 years ago and was probably earlier than that, but from where and by whom still remains to be answered. Pottery too appears in the archaeological record, but only briefly and in the early portion of it, before A.D. 500; this is a significant piece of information about traditional Kosraean material culture because at Contact, the Kosraeans had no indigenous pottery or pottery-making industry. Other information vital to our outline of the past includes the appearance of breadfruit and three aroid cultigens (*Colocasia*, *Cyrtosperma* and *Alocasia*) some 2,000 years ago (Athens 1995); all of which needed the intercession of a human hand to introduce these foreign plants to the shores of Kosrae. Even a shift in the regular exploitation of shellfish appears in the archaeological record, with an initial emphasis on bivalves before A.D. 500 and gastropods after that date.

But what about the people themselves? Precious little is known or has been tied to tangible evidence of their habits, their role in the establishment and spread of communities, the division of the island into regional districts, or their increasingly complex political-, economic- and social systems. Thus far, only the late period, Contact-era Kosraean has been portrayed in archaeological musings and interpretations. For those earlier eras, the human factor remains an abstract element in the total cultural equation. Yet, it was the prime contributor to the creation of the archaeological record; unfortunately, it also remains part of the background noise commonly encountered in any archaeological excavation.

The Early Years. In 1910, the German South Seas Expedition landed on the island to continue their scientific survey of Micronesian culture. The plan was for Ernst Sarfert to remain on-island for three months to complete an ethnographic investigation, while Paul Hambruch, an archaeologist with the Expedition, would remain only as long as the Expedition ship was in port, roughly two weeks. Hambruch coordinated the first systematic archaeological project to be conducted on the island. It took as its focus the historical site of Leluh, the 'other' monumental architectural site in this part of the Pacific, a rival to Pohnpei's Nan Madol. He had already gathered some information on Leluh from adventurers such as Frederick Christian (1899), who not only described the larger compounds in Leluh, but also described excavations into those compounds. Together, in what can only be described as a monumental effort stretching over a two week period, Hambruch and members of the Expedition began their work on Leluh (Figure 7 a,b).

The islet had been mostly abandoned for nearly a century by the time they began work. It was overrun with dense jungle, with the canals through the islet silted-in and choked with an impenetrable thicket of hibiscus. The meters high walls of the compounds, according to Hambruch (Sarfert 1919), were virtually invisible; you could not locate them either simply or easily. And it rained, almost continuously, with hours of long down pours during which no work could be completed. The final result of this effort, however, was an exceptionally thorough account of Leluh; it was a major achievement of value and interest (Sarfert 1919). Subsequent archaeological work on Leluh has merely added additional, qualitative information, changing little from the first descriptions and interpretations of Hambruch and Sarfert. Even the map produced from this first effort remains virtually intact, with only minor changes made by later investigations. The German Expedition established in what is truly an unsurpassed and unprecedented effort a foundation of knowledge for

Figure 7. Traditional architectural remains: a, b. Leluh, each of which display a common construction technique, with a boulder base topped by a columnar basalt header-stretcher pattern; c. single compound in Utwe (this was one of our other projects, but it is an example of a typical compound encountered in TT Times projects.

understanding Leluh, as well as the rest of Kosraean traditional culture.

Between 1914 and World War II, the Japanese government administered Kosrae, along with the rest of Micronesia, as part of their expanded territory. Each of the major islands in this new territory was the recipient of Japanese curiosity, and the subject of a limited series of archaeological investigations (Yawata 1930, 1932a, 1932b). Their scientists swarmed throughout Micronesia, documenting archaeological sites, collecting artifacts, and speculating on the origin of the peoples, often with attempts to link Japan to the islands as the point of cultural origin. Few of these studies, however, have been translated and remain inaccessible.

The outbreak of World War II brought an end to the Japanese investigations, and to all archaeological and scientific inquiries. Leluh became the site of a Japanese military installation, while Malem hosted most of the Japanese soldiers who were stationed on Kosrae in defense of the Japanese Empire. Various military facilities were constructed around the island; many of which have become a part of the archaeological record. It wasn't until the establishment of the Trust Territory administration after the war, when the United States assumed trusteeship of Kosrae and the rest of Micronesia under a United Nations mandate, that archaeological work began anew and with a new emphasis.

TT and CRM. Modern archaeological research on Kosrae began in the 1970s as part of the regional programs administered by the Historic Preservation

Office of the United States Trust Territory of the Pacific Islands. A number of archaeological projects were carried out under the direction of Ross Cordy, territorial archaeologist. Many of these projects were generated by major infrastructure development on the island, including road building, waterline installation, the construction of wastewater facilities, and other capital improvement projects. With each, a series of small, directed and systematic surveys were conducted, some of which required archaeological testing and excavation. Numerous sites were recorded, along with radiocarbon dates and a variety of other data needed to fill in the large gaps within the developing cultural outline for the island. Much of the cultural timeline seemed to focus on the later part of the pre-Contact era with Leluh as the principal reference point; this is, in part, a consequence of CRM (cultural resource management) driven research where infrastructure development becomes the determining factor in site selection, but it also reflects the initial historical focus of archaeological work on the island. This rather lopsided direction in archaeological investigation left the earliest sites and earliest eras untouched, or at least under-reported. When they actually did become the subject of archaeological inquiry, e.g., Likinlulem, the stage had already been set; unless an early era site could be directly related to the rise and development of Leluh, it was dismissed as a quaint provincial locale of little consequence, a mere stepping stone in the path to Leluh (Figure 7).

The first projects in TT Times, as the era of trusteeship is often referred, consisted of both surveys and data recoveries for infrastructure development (Craib 1978, Cordy 1981, 1983, Sinoto 1982). Other projects within the same general time included a major intensive survey, mapping and testing effort directed at Leluh, in effect redoing the work of Hambruch et al. some 70 years prior (Cordy 1982a, 1982b, 1985, 1993, Morgan 1988). Other archaeological work at Leluh included more infrastructure related projects by Bath (1986), Bath and Shun (1982), and Athens (1995). Additional, extra-Leluh archaeological work was concentrated on the island's coastal plain, and included efforts in Okat, Innem, Loal (Lacl), Utwe, Likinlulem, and Malem (Bath, Shun and Cordy 1983, Cordy 1983, Cordy et al. 1985, Athens et al. 1983, Welch et al. 1990, Swift et al. 1990).

One of the extra-Leluh investigations is particularly relevant to the Safonfok investigation—the archaeological survey and excavation of Likinlulem (Bath, Shun and Cordy 1983), one of the most significant historical sites on Kosrae, at least according to oral histories. But, according to the Territorial archaeologist at the time, the lack of monumentality at Likinlulem was sufficient to dismiss the site as a major influence in the cultural development of the island (Cordy 1982b, 1993). Yet, it is the one site on the island that appears regularly (and in a key role) in legendary histories, including the mythical stories detailing the formation of various geographical features that make up the island. It was the place from which traditional titles originated, and is said to have housed the island's highest chiefs with the oldest lineages, at least until about A.D. 1400, when the rival site of Leluh became the seat of the paramountcy and ushered in a new era of political complexity. Likinlulem is frequently described as having been occupied 'before time began' or 'before the before,' in much the same way Safonfok has been described (see below). According to the results of archaeological investigations, Likinlulem was occupied by about A.D. 1000 (and likely even earlier), with its peak period of occupation between about A.D. 1200 and 1600—a time frame that is becoming increasingly important in the history of Kosrae, and one which makes Likinlulem a contemporary to Safonfok.

In 1987 the Trust Territory era ended. Kosrae became one of four states within the newly independent Federated States of Micronesia. However, independence from U.S. administration did not stem the effort of historic preservation or archaeological research. It still continues today, with much of the work now conducted by the direct ancestors of the earliest settlers to the island.

# III. RESEARCH OBJECTIVES, GOALS AND STRATEGIES

No one would dream of making an experimental contribution to physical or chemical science, without giving a detailed account of all the arrangements of the experiments; an exact description of the apparatus used; of the manner in which the observations were conducted; of their number; of the length of time devoted to them, and of the degree of approximation with which each measurement was made. In less exact sciences, as in biology or geology, this cannot be done as rigorously, but every student will do his best to bring home to the reader all the conditions in which the experiment or the observations were made. [Malinowski 1984]

So began Malinowski's advice to would-be ethnographers in his 1922 landmark monograph, *Argonauts of the Western Pacific*. It is essentially a guidebook to the research process, intended to instill an appreciation for the need to produce candid accounts of data collection and interpretation during fieldwork. It is, he continues, the responsibility of every researcher to provide sufficient information so that others can replicate the process and reproduce the results. Such universal advice is applicable to any discipline that uses as its mainstay exploration and observation in the collection of data and its subsequent interpretation. The following pages take their cue from Malinowski. They present a description of the methods and research objectives used to investigate, document and interpret the historical site of Safonfok in all its sundry dimensions: surface, subsurface, place in the physical and cultural landscape, context within local and regional prehistories and chronologies, and significance relative to the historical record of Kosrae and the region (entry onto the U.S. National Register of Historic Places is one means by which significance is assigned, and was one of the tasks requested for project outcomes).

Our discussion begins with an outline of the fundamental research domains that have been used to direct the context and content of this investigation. Each defines a 'reference point' or signpost in a field of infinite possibilities, guiding the development of new paradigms or tools well adapted to severing the Gordian knots of traditional histories in Kosrae and the Pacific. The principal goal is, afterall, interpretation of the archaeological record and the attendant history it represents. As broadly defined, history becomes a moving target, represented by a multitude of voices, attitudes and perspectives. The past is not a fixed, permanent entity, but harbors a content represented by selective fragments of events and activities that have withstood the ravages of time. The preponderance of this 'evidence,' the surviving remnants of the past, is filtered still further by the shifting perspectives of oral historians,

archaeologists and ethnographic historians. Of course, context also plays an important role in the recognition of 'evidence,' particularly as there are no eyewitness accounts upon which to rely.

In archaeology, or any other discipline for that matter, we tend to be selective in our accounts of the past, emphasizing one set of materials while ignoring another. We are, afterall, only human, and as such we are also born storytellers. Each of our voices represents a discrete perspective that focuses on and pursues different interpretations of the events in history. And, when the voice, or teller, changes, so does the content of that history. Our narratives of the past will be, by their very nature, incomplete simply because the act of 'telling' requires elaborating upon some elements and silencing others. This is an active process that for fields like archaeology requires establishment of guidelines, often presented in the form of a research design. Only in this manner can an overzealous, enthusiast of the past be constrained and made to focus on the task at hand—developing a comprehensive, organized, foundation-building description of the past. The process begins by focusing on material remains, fixing a context for their presence in space and time; only afterwards will an expanded estimation, interpretation and narration of their position within the larger realms of social, political and economic systems make sense.

## Research Design

Archaeological research is not conducted in a vacuum. Nearly any history of our discipline will demonstrate that explaining the past has been a major part of archaeology since its inception (Bell 1994, Trigger 1989, Willey and Sabloff 1980). But that explanation must, by necessity, be directed through a series of filters; a context of salient research domains that can render a host of unassimilated field and laboratory data into a comprehensible whole. From this tangled web of facts and material evidence, a significant narrative emerges to define and describe past human events and processes that have left their mark in the archaeological record of the region.

Research domains developed for the historic site of Safonfok speak to basic archaeological tasks, such as the establishment of local chronologies, patterns of material consumption and the continuing definition of settlement patterns and site types. But they also go beyond these to more complex issues of regional settlement models, land use patterns, growing political and social complexity across the island, distribution and control over technology and manufacturing industries, the enigmatic and restricted appearance of pottery, subsistence practices, and even issues of past environments and biotic communities. Each of these issues, themes, topics and domains are part of a larger pattern of inquiry into the past life, history and environment across Kosrae. They are also instrumental in establishing a context for comprehension and offer guidance in the development of an overall research design, field strategies and ultimately evaluation of site significance.

It is always tempting to adjust your recollection of the attitudes and intent that were called into focus during the initial planning stages of any archaeological investigation. At the ready is the benefit of hindsight, ruminations about how you would do something a little different 'had you only known.' There is a conscious temptation, and a subconscious tendency, to smooth away the difficulties, to synthesize and consolidate them, and to express them as disinterested research arenas ripe for investigation. In spite of this, it is still important to sort out past notions from present ideas, and to record just what was in mind at the onset of investigation. We knew very little about Safonfok initially, only that it was large and had no associated oral history relating its significance or role within the traditional history. But, we did know there were several pressing issues in Kosrae's history to which investigations at the site could contribute. With this in mind, the following issues or themes were developed.

## Chronology

Several radiocarbon dates have been derived from historical sites across Kosrae, but their collection integrity, context and association have proven problematical. During the Wastewater Project, Athens (1995) reevaluated all the radiocarbon dates generated prior to his work on the island and essentially invalidated may of them. The remaining dates (perhaps surviving would be a better term) were integrated into those derived from the Wastewater Project to produce an overall chronology of occupation on the island. While large gaps remain in this sequence, an overall pattern did emerge; one that included occupation on Kosrae about A.D. 100, with indications in the data that occupation and possibly initial settlement of the island could have occurred earlier, sometime between the first centuries B.C. and A.D. (Athens 1995).

In his ever-thorough manner, Athens described at least three discrete spikes in the radiocarbon curve produced by the collection of secure dates, with each spike indicating a clustering or density of dates. About A.D. 500, the density of dates radically increases; another dramatic jump in the curve occurs between A.D. 800 and 1200; a third spike is observed between A.D. 1250 and 1450. Athens (1995) suggests the increase in the density of radiocarbon dates could reflect major population increases, although he also suggested that these could be the result of excavation bias or an artifact of the radiocarbon curve. From his own work on the Wastewater Project, Athens (1995) sees indications in the archaeological record of an initial spread of small groups of people after A.D. 500, with A.D. 1200 marking a point in time in which open land was filled and changes in political organization, i.e., increasing complexity, occurred.

This particular issue—the establishment of a secure chronology of settlement and occupation—has a direct bearing on many other major research questions concerning Micronesian prehistory: origins, linguistics, models of island settlement, population movement, and so on. Early dates from the region include roughly 2,000 year old dates from the Marshall Islands (Shun and Athens 1990, Beardsley 1994), Pohnpei and Chuuk (Athens 1990, Shutler 1984, Weisler 2001), but what of Kosrae? The work of Athens (1995) has pushed back the time of occupation on-island, but does it reflect initial settlement? So far, the data is not there, but it is a start. Unfortunately, just having an early date or two from a single site means little; what is needed is a secure series of radiocarbon dates from many sites.

Large gaps in the island chronology remain. A substantial collection of dates from Safonfok could prove to be a boon for this chronology, and may help fill in some of those gaps, especially those in the pre-Leluh era.

## Material Culture: Patterns of Consumption, Technology and Manufacturing Industries

Material culture remains and their associated industries tell us much about the inner workings of a culture and its supporting communities. They serve as a symbol, representing cultural activities and affiliations, embodying new ideas and the diffusion of ideas; they are what lead us to understand traditional era economic, social and political organization on an island. The full range of material cultural studies contributes both spatially and temporally to our understanding of daily, seasonal and perhaps annual activities and routines, patterns of trade and interaction, the growth and movement of populations, the expansion and contraction of regional polities, possible alliances within and between polities, and shifting patterns of consumption, access and the distribution of resources.

According to Athens (1995), there is no archaeological evidence for inter-island (or even intra-island) contact with Kosrae following initial settlement. But what would that evidence look like? The dearth of artifacts recovered from the combined archaeological investigations of the past has yet to provide us with even a brief sketch of past cultural practices and lifeways. Much of our current knowledge is based on analogies drawn from ethnohistorical observations and archaeological accounts of other Micronesian high islands.

There is very little written about local production industries visible in the archaeological record on-island, including the manufacture of that ubiquitous Pacific Island artifact—the adze—as well as beads, fishhooks, canoes, and so on. Even more glaringly absent is, or rather was, the presence of pottery. Athens (1995) and the Wastewater Project addressed this conundrum: over 200 sherds of a locally made pottery dating between the first centuries B.C. and A.D. were recovered from deeply submerged deposits on the island of Leluh. In fortuitous fits and starts, a scattered picture of life in the past, as represented by material culture elements, is gradually building for Kosrae. But this is an agonizingly slow process. The recovery of even a modicum of artifacts and their accompanying production industries could provide a significant addition to the history of occupation and activities on the island.

Pottery. Pottery was unknown in the archaeological record on Kosrae until the Wastewater Project (Athens 1995). This project marks the first recorded recovery of such a rare, but highly anticipated artifact. The pottery fragments had been recovered from deep deposits along Kosrae's coastal margins, which is perhaps one reason it had not been encountered previously; natural sedimentation along with artificial fill on Leluh had covered the deposits. Its limited occurrence in time too was perhaps another reason, as it is confined to a few hundred years prior to A.D. 500. After that date, pottery is no longer encountered in the archaeological record.

The few hundred sherds that were recovered tended to be quite fragmented. Most displayed distinctly rounded edges and had an eroded appearance, as if water-rolled in a low energy surf zone. Athens (1995) described it as comparable to other Pacific island pottery. There are no manufacturing marks, like thumb or finger indentations, coil remnants, paddle and anvil marks, or carbon residues. Nor are they any indications of decoration. Temper too is variable; some had no temper, some appeared to have calcareous sand temper, and in some there is a small amount of gravel-sized basaltic materials included in the clay matrix (this was probably fortuitous rather than a deliberate addition).

From the few surviving fragments of Kosraean pottery sherds, the vessels appear to have a limited number of rim forms, each distinct enough to place Kosraean pottery into a category of its own in this part of the Pacific. Relatively largish body sherds suggested at least some vessels had very distinctive angular side walls, while another fragment represented a carinated bowl with a thin rim. In still other instances, rims suggested vessel shapes with outward flaring forms and squared lips. Angled side walls, along with squared-off rims are found on Chuuk, as are carinated vessel forms. However, no similar forms appear on Pohnpei, the closest high island to Kosrae. Initially, the pottery on Kosrae was thought to fall within the range of the Late Lapita Plain Ware tradition; further still, that it could not be derived from older pottery traditions in the Mariana Islands or island southeast Asia (Athens 1995). Up to this point, archaeological and linguistic evidence have pointed to an origin of Kosrae settlers somewhere in the Lapita homeland, in the southeast Solomon Islands and the New Hebrides region. Yet the pottery forms recovered by Athens suggest an independent design element, rather than something derivative of these southern regions. How does this correlate with other elements of material culture?

## Settlement Models and Site Types

Patterns of settlement and the spatial distribution of archaeological site types are key to establishing an estimate of hierarchy among physical places, which in turn is directly tied to levels of site importance. What were the functions of these differing levels? Are there distinct differences in site size and style? Does environmental setting correlate with site hierarchy? An overall settlement definition is among one of the more pressing problems for the island. Once we gain a better grasp of this aspect of social and political organization as it has been expressed through time, we will be in a better position to proceed onto a host of other problems or issues. Was Safonfok, for example, strategically located in a position that related to defense? If it was a high ranking administrative site owing to its size, what were its rivals, and did its rivals share many of the same features? Excavations at Safonfok may not be able to address the full range of potential questions related to political power and social organization, but it does offer the opportunity to add to our basic knowledge, especially of the pre-Leluh era.

Previous archaeological surveys have indicated a traditional/prehistoric settlement pattern in which most sites are located along the narrow coastal plain and within the larger valleys. It is a pattern of dispersed residential structures consisting of either isolated enclosures or small clusters of enclosures. They often contain cobble pavements, though sometimes the pavements are isolated and not associated with any other site or feature. The assumption has been that pavements, whether isolated or not, are house foundations; although these assumptions have yet to be verified.

Enclosures are roughly rectangular in shape and range greatly in size. Walls will vary in height and thickness, but usually consist of basalt and coral (the latter used mainly in close proximity to the shoreline) boulders and cobbles. There may or may not be pavements in center of the enclosures, and in some instances there may be a raised or stacked platform. Other features associated with enclosures, especially residential sites, include assemblages of burned and cracked rock, charcoal, and charcoal stained soil. Artifacts often observed and recovered in and near enclosures include *seka* pounding stones, and food pounding and (occasionally) medicine pounding stones, but few other artifacts. Vegetation cover too complicates recognition of architectural features; pavements are particularly difficult to identify as they are not only covered with vegetation, but sometimes with a layer of soil as well.

At least four very large site complexes have been recorded around the island, excluding the artificial island complex of Leluh. Each of these complexes—Nefalil, Likinlulem, Yacl, and Lacl—consist of eight or more enclosures and range in date from A.D. 1200 to 1400 (Welch et al. 1990). The most common archaeological interpretation, expressed by Cordy and Ueki (1983) and Cordy (1985), suggests these large sites served as autonomous administrative centers and the residences of high chiefs prior to the consolidation of political authority at Leluh, when high chiefs were then obliged to live at Leluh and not in their home districts.

Another, often neglected element in settlement studies is recognition of important, extra-residential site types such as terraces, slope retaining walls, field alignments, and gardens. Such features are noticeably absent from archaeological survey identifications. Heavy vegetation growth and perhaps gentle sloping terrain on the narrow coastal plain are not conducive to the preservation of terraces, for example; if they are visible at all, they may simply look like a low platform or the edge of a buried pavement. Other fundamental difficulties in identification also persist and include the manner of construction. Many of these features have been continually rebuilt, modified and even moved over the course of their lifetimes, which makes them more vulnerable to the forces of nature. There are also no consistent descriptions as to what these features may have looked like, or the kinds of activities or artifacts that may be associated with them. Perhaps investigations at Safonfok can contribute some clarification to this issue.

## Increasing Complexity and Shifting Land Use Patterns

At what point do we begin to document increasing social complexity and island unification? Much of the discussion has centered on the rise of Leluh, mainly when it was constructed and the interpretation of radiocarbon dates associated with the site (Graves 1986, Cordy 1982a,b, Athens 1995). But what is the social and cultural foundation upon which Leluh consolidated its power? Was this the first real move toward a more

complex social organization on the island? Or were their other episodes or attempts at consolidation and the formation of a centralized powerbase to administer an increasingly complicated and complex population? Any discussion of increasing complexity and shifting land use patterns are directly tied to settlement models and site definition, as well as chronology. They are based on expectations of human/land relationships, which are, however, infused with many variables and unknowns that have yet to be resolved.

## Subsistence Practices

This has been a somewhat neglected area of study, but one also fraught with a number of difficulties including inconsistent analyses of midden deposits, their intensity of use, duration, and composition; differential preservation of tangible remains, mainly terrestrial and marine faunal remains as opposed to agricultural remains, along with the tools that accompany each mode of capture, preparation and consumption. Athens (1995) tried to address this very issue as part of the Wastewater Project; up to then, archaeological investigations merely provided lists of excavated shellfish remains, as if there were no other components within the subsistence regimen. Ritter and Ritter (1982), however, present several documentary sources that describe the importance of breadfruit and other food plants—banana, coconut, pandanus, yam, sugarcane. Shellfish was but a minor part of the overall diet, according to these sources.

In his work, Athens (1995) was able to show an early emphasis on bivalve exploitation before A.D. 500, after that gastropods seem to dominate the shellfish record. This same pattern of shellfish exploitation is visible in the archaeological record of the Mariana Islands (Athens 1995), although no such pattern has been documented on Pohnpei, the closest high island in this part of the Pacific. Athens (1995) also demonstrated that the presence and abundance of bone in excavated remains paints a very different picture; one that indicates fish were by far the most abundant vertebrate resource utilized for all time periods. No temporal trends could be discerned in the fish remains, and as for non-fish remains, they were minimal. An analysis of the fishbone showed a preference for the exploitation of a wide variety of nearshore and shallow water species, i.e., reef fish. Surgeon fish, trigger fish, wrasses, and parrot fish were among the most commonly exploited taxa. The remains of pelagic fish were minimal for all time periods.

A small amount of dog bone was associated with the prehistoric occupation; it does not appear in historic era contexts nor was the presence of dog reported at Contact. Rat, sheep or goat, pig, cat, and toad also occur in minimal amounts in the excavated remains, but they are only associated with the historic era. The absence of pig in the prehistoric record fits the general pattern of absence throughout Micronesia, with exception of Palau and Fais (Masse et al. 1984, Intoh 1986, 1996).

The general dominance of marine-oriented subsistence remains in archaeological deposits throughout the island is not necessarily a measure of their role in the basic economy; it is more likely a function of differential preservation. Compared to marine exploitation, cultivation tools and products in particular leave little behind in the archaeological record. The recovery and analysis of subsistence remains at Safonfok is not expected to produce significant alterations to the existing information, but it can provide support and confirmation to these observations, and potentially contribute toward establishment of temporal change in subsistence patterns as well as possible variation in subsistence patterns between sites.

**Environmental Precursors**

This issue is really about landscape and vegetation changes, and the determination of natural versus cultural or humanly induced changes. How much of the landscape, for example, is the result of human interference and modification? Few researchers in Micronesia have dealt with this question (Hunter-Anderson 2002, Athens 1995), yet this is a critical issue in understanding local adaptation to an island environment, and the kinds of geomorphological and vegetation changes that have occurred over time. What plants are indigenous? Which were introduced? What is the source of the introduced plants? What plants, animals or habitat have been extirpated or became extinct as a result of human activity? Also of interest is evidence of sea level change, possible climate change, geomorphological change, and the role each played in the formation and evolution of the island environment.

Part of the Wastewater Project investigations was focused on non-archaeological sites, with an eye toward documenting an environmental history of the island (Athens 1995). At about A.D. 500, sediment cores indicate an increasing abundance of charcoal, which has been interpreted as the residues of land clearing efforts by island occupants; there was, the interpretation continues, intense forest burning at this time, all around the island. Also indicated within these cores was a period of localized slope erosion and infilling, which is likely linked to the large scale burning. Pollen diagrams further support an interpretation of the disappearance of native lowland forest at this time, with the island landscape transformed into an agroforest dominated by breadfruit, coconut and other food trees important in subsistence regimes.

Additional findings from the Wastewater Project indicate that sediment core dates from wetland swamps show an expansion of mangrove forests roughly between A.D. 500 and 1000, and up to about A.D. 1300. Prior to this time, swamplands were shallow open water lagoons with marine sands and detritus on the bottom. They were protected from the open sea by a barrier berm that formed about 3,000 years ago as a result of falling sea level. Was the shift to wetland swamps the result of human manipulation? Perhaps a result of the expansion of agricultural lands? This may be one factor among many; other work by Athens (1995) indicates a falling sea level at this time, with modern levels reached about A.D. 1100 to 1300. With a gradual drop in sea level, water circulation in the lagoon areas would have been reduced, creating favorable habitat for the growth and expansion of mangrove forests. Perhaps the Safonfok excavations can contribute additional information and insights into this emerging picture of landscape change in both time and space across the island.

*Field Methods*

Fieldwork is the means by which we collect sufficient data to address the research domains described above. It is the practical application of our sampling strategy, a fundamental part of any research project that represents the first control on the quality of all subsequent analyses and decisions based on those data (Richardson 1993). And as proxy for the site of Safonfok in all its dimensions, the archaeological sample becomes the basic source of information for all analyses, interpretations and inferences. It must result in the recovery of sufficient data to address three basic questions:

- Is the sample large enough to represent the archaeological deposit within the site?

- Does the sample possess many of the same characteristics as the site deposit?

- Will the data generated from the sample represent the entire site deposit, in all its dimensions?

With this weighty responsibility placed upon our shoulders, the fieldwork was divided into three basic tasks: a) intensive reconnaissance, clearing and mapping of all surface architecture, features, artifact deposits and other culturally significant deposits; b) placement and completion of stratigraphy trenches; and, c) controlled excavation in selected areas of the site. The actual fieldwork consisted of detailed observations, maps, records, and photographs of the site, its features and each excavation area; surface collections; random, fortuitous reconnaissance forays beyond the immediate site area; and basic botanical and geological surveys intended to establish an environmental context for the site. Throughout the entire duration of fieldwork, we found ourselves dodging falling breadfruit and coconuts, as both plants had been cultivated within the site boundaries some time after its abandonment.

All excavations, trenches and surface features were mapped with a compass, a surveyors level, elevation rod, and 30-meter tape. Individual datum points were established for each excavation area; while excavation forms and notes, photographs, stratigraphic profiles, and descriptions were completed for all subsurface exposures. Every sample, whether artifact or specialized sample, was assigned a unique lot designation or provenience. This singular reference serves as the only link between the original location of the sampled materials and the fieldwork, laboratory analyses and interpretation, and subsequent archival storage.

## Clearing and Reconnaissance

During each season of fieldwork, our time in the field was relatively short. As such, fieldwork was necessarily intensive, demanding that a variety of tasks be conducted concurrently (Figures 8 to 10). The first task was to define the approximate extent of the site, which was accomplished with a superficial sweep through the area hanging colored flagging tape at the limits of surface exposures of architectural and structural features, as well as artifact scatters and midden deposits. After which, the crew was divided, with a portion dedicated to brush clearing and the remainder put to work identifying all exposed archaeological features and deposits related to the site.

In a place where the jungle vegetation is marked by luxuriant growth, a singular transect through the bush means crawling under and through thickets, diverting your passage around a cluster of impenetrable brush, and crawling over vines and other ground cover that places you well above the ground surface. Under these conditions, ground visibility is severely limited, and spatial orientation of archaeological materials to site features is hampered. Brush clearing was the order of the day. Armed with machetes, a portion of the archaeological crew set to work felling brush and other pioneering plants that take advantage of disturbed environments. This process, however, tends to further obscure the ground surface by burying it beneath an ankle-deep layer of cut foliage. Clearing work then, is completed in at least two stages: machete work to fell the brush and hack it into smaller segments, followed by stacking the brush in piles throughout the site with an eye toward leaving visible artifact deposits and archaeological features exposed for further examination.

Reconnaissance surveys were conducted both within and outside the site area (as defined by the compound wall) along parallel transects spaced roughly 5 meters apart. Inside the compound wall, the survey transect took on the form of a grid pattern, with a second set of transects conducted perpendicular to the first. Outside the compound, transects remained parallel to the compound wall. Every artifact and archaeological feature encountered over the course of this search pattern was immediately flagged. During the subsequent mapping work, each flag and the feature or artifact(s) it marked was then systematically numbered and recorded.

Surveyors took advantage of crab burrows, pig wallows and their excavations to indicate possible subsurface deposits and features. Such fortuitous exposures added another dimension to the surface record, and provided valuable information when it came time to position excavation units.

At the end of each field season, the final task was to collect selected surface artifacts identified during this reconnaissance (and after they had been mapped in place). This was incorporated into the overall housecleaning chores for the site, which also included backfilling excavation units, pulling up flagging and mapping stakes, and collecting any trash left on the site over the course of fieldwork.

## Mapping

A detailed, accurate map is basic to all investigations at the site. There are two basic techniques that were contemplated, both of which produced plans at the scale and accuracy demanded. One technique makes use of a plane table, on which the map takes shape under your very gaze during the course of the survey; the other relies on the use of an instrument such as a transit or surveyors level with angle plate, and requires that the map be plotted afterward from numerical data.

Figure 8. Field mapping.

For most archaeological maps, the plane table is an ideal choice. The advantage is that problems concerning the way a feature is represented become apparent immediately, and can be resolved on the spot; another is that gaps in coverage are unlikely to occur (Willey et al. 1975). But, one advantage a transit or level has over a plane table is that scale becomes flexible. The numerical data generated by this technique can be plotted at any scale, depending on the requirements attached to specific project needs.

Certainly, a point can be more quickly plotted on the plane table than entered into a notebook and later translated onto paper with protractor and ruler. And, errors in reading angles, elevation or distances go unnoticed until the map is put down on paper. But, the short duration of each field season, coupled with the additional fieldwork demands that require the participation of every crew member, meant very little time could be spent plotting a map in the field. In an effort to minimize at least the blatant blunders and lacunae, the site was systematically mapped in overlapping sections.

Figure 9. Laying out a unit block.

Mapping was completed with a compass, a surveyors level with an angle plate, an elevation rod, and a 30-meter tape. A series of datum points were established at strategically located points from which an area with a 30-meter radius could be covered. Prior to any mapping work, numbered stakes were laid out in the immediate mapping section. They were used to demarcate the twists and turns, corners, interior and exterior points of the variety of archaeological features occurring within that particular area. Excavation units and stratigraphic trenches were mapped, as were individual artifacts, midden deposits, and breadfruit trees (to review their overall cultivation pattern). By the time mapping work was completed, the site was awash with a sea flags.

Each datum point was directly tied to the preceding datum, with a compass reading, angle and distance measured between the two. Additionally, magnetic north was established for each datum point. A site map was started during the evening hours, with the expectation that any irregularities might be caught before we left the field. When errors or irregularities were highlighted in this process, it was a fairly easy matter to return to that datum and erroneous point and correct the distance and angle measurements.

## Stratigraphic Trenches

Upon completion of the surface survey, specific areas within the site were chosen for stratigraphic exposures. These were placed in areas that exhibited an absence of identified cultural deposits such as middens or surface scatter of artifacts. Stratigraphic trenches are simply that; a mechanism to establish and examine stratigraphic sequences across the site, with an eye toward ascertaining the stratigraphic relationship of each area of the site. The only real requirement in completing the trench was definition of its lateral extent; each trench was no more than 2-meters long. Subsequent recording tasks were then routine from start to finish: excavation of the trench; definition, description and record of the stratigraphy following an established procedure; measured profile drawings of the stratigraphic sequences visible on trench walls. As Sir Mortimer Wheeler stated, it is scarcely necessary to add that the utility of such a record . . . is proportionate to the accuracy of the measured section or sections with which the record is subsequently to be equated (Wheeler 1955).

All faces of the trench were examined, as no two sides of a trench are exactly identical. Each stratum was then described following standardized descriptions that took into account such characteristics as texture, structure, mottling, the presence of roots, artifacts, charcoal, midden, and even beach-building parent materials. Soil color was described using Munsell color notation charts. Each stratigraphic layer was temporarily numbered until all stratigraphic profiles could be examined. Only then were permanent layer designations assigned to each stratum. Sublayer designations, denoted by an alphabetic indicator (e.g., IIIa or IVb), were occasionally used when soil layers were similar except for minor variations in color, texture, or matrix.

The stratigraphic trench is almost like a control-pit, in that it provides a record of the nature and probable vertical extent of each stratum. It is like a glimpse into the future, forming a model from which to work and, more importantly, avoid confusion about the lower part of one stratum and the upper part of the next underlying stratum. It also serves as the primary referent for the site deposit, illustrating the transitional depth of diffusion and mixing between layers, and a geological brief of the landform history. Without a stratigraphic trench, excavation would proceed blindly, perhaps expending precious time and resources excavating to depths well below cultural deposits.

## Controlled Excavations

The basic unit of excavation was the one-meter square grid unit, although some flexibility was built into this system to accommodate odd-shaped areas. All excavation units were placed within or nearby architectural features and areas of the site that exhibited heavy usage or dense occupation. This latter was determined by the spatial clustering of artifacts and cultural deposits, such as midden, on the site surface, as well as the range and variety of artifacts brought to the surface by crabs. In 1999, excavation units were used predominately to test the integrity of subsurface deposits in those areas where surface features and artifact densities suggested concentrated activity; in 2001, excavation units were consigned to blocks which were placed in the more productive 1999 areas, as well as in areas where intensive living activities were suggested, such as heavy kitchen use or areas dedicated to manufacturing activities. Unit numbers were assigned consecutively, beginning with Units 1 to 6 excavated in 1999, and continuing with Units 7 to 28 during the 2001 field season.

Unit/block orientation was predominately toward magnetic north, unless the area selected for excavation presented immovable obstacles (especially closely spaced trees) that required accommodation. A reference datum was established at each unit/block; each block consisted of several conjoined units, each of which was excavated individually in order to control provenience. Prior to any excavation, surface depth below (or above) datum was measured and recorded. This provided a useful beginning point from which excavation could proceed systematically, in regular 10-centimeter levels. Hand excavation techniques were employed, that is manually digging with trowels, hand picks, brushes, and dustpans. Nearly all excavations were terminated within the first 10-cm of the culturally sterile stratum underlying the principal site deposit. At least one unit in each block excavation was dug to greater depths, extending to the active beach layer that seems to mark the initial geological deposit for this particular landform. All information generated for each level was recorded on standardized grid forms.

Excavated sediments were screened through 1/4-inch wire mesh, with the exception of one unit, Unit 12. The sediments from this single unit were screened through 1/8-inch wire mesh in an effort to develop comparative information on recovery differences based on screen size. All recognizable artifacts, including charcoal and bone, were sorted and bagged separately during screening of all units, with the remainder of the excavated screen residue bagged in bulk for additional sorting in the laboratory. Features encountered during excavation were sampled separately, especially if they were tentatively identified as hearths or secondary ash deposits. Each feature was recorded on excavation plan maps and subsequent wall profiles. A bulk sample of the matrix was removed from the *in situ* feature.

Excavation blocks and individual units were photographed over the course of excavation.

Stratigraphic profiles were drawn from at least two walls in each excavation block, while stratigraphic descriptions, including Munsell color notations, were recorded on standardized forms.

Tarpaulins were used to protect the crew from the rain, and to insure that work continued even during inclement periods of weather. The tarps were placed over active excavation blocks, screening areas and the mapping instrument position. Each crew took on the responsibility of erecting the tents as needed, utilizing local materials for structural supports.

Figure 10. Drawing unit profile.

## Laboratory Methods

Fieldwork is simply the first of two stages in the collection of a large array of data recruited in the quest for answers to questions currently asked, and those which may be asked in the future about the life and times of occupation at Safonfok. The second, complementary stage is the laboratory. It is the phase where the past unfolds in a level of detail generally not visible in the heat of fieldwork. Laboratory methods are more or less systematized, with only minor variation where necessary. All lab work begins and ends with constant reference to the sample lot designation created in the field; this singular reference is the only link between fieldwork and the original location of excavated materials.

During fieldwork, an outdoor laboratory was set up. Here, as time permitted, bulk screen residues were sorted by material type, with immediately recognizable artifacts, charcoal and bone bagged separately. This raw sorting was in preparation for the more intensive procedures to be completed at the close of fieldwork, when artifacts would be measured, weighed, classified and described. Charcoal samples would be selected for radiocarbon dating; and bone, wood charcoal, coral, and shell samples would be sent to appropriate laboratories for identification. Field sorting actually expedited the overall laboratory treatment process, as it allowed analysis to begin almost immediately.

Artifacts were washed, sorted and assigned unique catalog numbers. Each was measured, weighed and classified, with both metric and descriptive attributes recorded. Analysis was primarily descriptive, with identifications and functional assessments augmented by information drawn from a variety of references, such as Buck (1957), Barrera and Kirch (1973), Kirch (1979), Sinoto (1979), and Emory, Bonk and Sinoto (1968).

Bone samples were submitted to Dr. Alan Ziegler for identification. Once identified, each category of faunal remains were counted and weighed. Selected fragments of wood charcoal and charred plant remains were sent to the Wood Identification Laboratory, Hawai'i, for identification. And potential dating samples recovered *in situ* and during the processing of bulk screen residues were submitted to the Radiocarbon Dating Laboratory at University of Waikato and Rafter Radiocarbon Laboratory.

## *Oral History*

As companion to the recovery of field data and the development of laboratory analyses, the collection of oral histories has become an integral part of any historical investigation in the Pacific. In fact, no archaeological investigation would be complete without an oral history component. It supplements the material assemblages, tendering meaning to an often skimpy archaeological record. It also provides the explanations and supplies those intangible qualities that cannot be recovered through archaeological techniques. But, the collection of oral histories is no easy task. Knowledge, especially of history or the social arts, represents both power and a commodity; it is a bargaining chip in cultural negotiations, with access restricted to a select few. As such, it is a domain perennially plagued by such questions as: Who is the recognized authority within a specific region? How much information can be solicited? Is the information received valid, reliable and relatively free of personal or political agendas? And, can confirmation be obtained from other unrelated authorities?

Oral histories are fluid, flexible narratives that are shaped anew by each generation. A story, any story, appears in many variations, with no one variant considered the 'true' version. Oral history in general serves to mediate knowledge of the past, as well as to provide the organizational diagrams necessary to understand the complicated actions of one's ancestors (Parmentier 1987). When applied to the archaeological record, it becomes an invaluable tool by providing a context and an understanding of the motivations behind the social structure responsible for the material remains. History, at least in the Pacific, is also a dynamic process that focuses on significant cultural and natural events, as well as relationships between various kin groups (Borowfski 2000). In the West, history takes a more linear approach, events are reckoned in a compounding progressive sequence that is affixed to a chronological order. The mere act of recording a history, including oral histories, in the Pacific is almost counter-intuitive, as it effectively freezes the form and content of the story, and does not provide for ways to incorporate the necessary changes and modifications that each story undergoes with time.

The oral history component of the Safonfok project was somewhat informal, and more of a reconnaissance rather than a full-fledged, formal systematic process. The lack of information within ethnohistoric sources, where Safonfok is no more than a place name without historical or cultural significance, offered little promise for the recovery of additional information that may be harbored in the minds and hearts of local historians. This, compounded with the continuing loss of oral traditions on the island as a whole, owing to the death of a number of local historians, led us to wonder what, if any, kind of information we may encounter. So, to test the proverbial waters, our inquiry into the oral history of Safonfok consisted of casual interviews conducted during the 2001 field season by a combined team of the Kosrae historic preservation staff and select members of the field crew. The interviews were conducted in Kosraean, with conversations allowed to wander over various topics according to the predilection of those interviewed. No tape recordings were made, and cryptic notes on the content of these conversations were rapidly recorded outside the presence of those interviewed. On the whole, the interviewers and the oral history project were well received and supported; there seems to have been little reticence in supplying information.

# IV. ARCHAEOLOGICAL FIELD INVESTIGATIONS

Our initial investigations at Safonfok were to be the last excavations of the 1999 field crew, and part of a final exam, so to speak, on their archaeological proficiency in both field method and interpretation. It was the end of our field season and the last site we would excavate together. This was to be their opportunity to demonstrate their abilities and to really shine in the application of freshly honed skills. They were in the spotlight, and they knew it. Safonfok was to be their last hurdle as it presented a new level of difficulty that would stretch their skills to the limit and require some improvisation in field strategies. All we knew about the site at the time was that it consisted of an extensive wall that had collapsed; it was an unknown place in local histories; and, there was no internal architecture. It was, for all intents, considered a highly disturbed site with little significance. How much information would the crew be able to recover from the site? Would they be able to determine the extent of the disturbance? Would they be able to reconstruct the series of events that contributed to the overall content and composition of the site, from its initial abandonment at an undetermined time in the past until today? Would they be able to retrieve any information on the timing, activities and organization of the site at the time it was occupied?

The preceding year, as part of the development permit review process, the KHPO archaeological staff had briefly visited Safonfok and mapped its wall. Dense vegetation, coupled with the tidal cycle, precluded any extensive or intensive examination of the compound's interior, other than a singular passage across its breadth, from one wall to another. If there had been any standing architectural feature within the compound interior, the expectation was that there would have been at least a hint of its presence. Experience at other sites on-island had already demonstrated that vegetation, no matter how dense, does not completely obscure a standing wall or platform. High tide too played a role in this initial 1998 mapping reconnaissance, as it dictated both the arrival and departure times for the archaeologists, cutting short exploration time and minimizing the number of days a boat would have to be hired for the passage.

This then, was the context under which our first field season at Safonfok began. The crew was expected to interpret the archaeological record at an historical site that was considered disturbed, that stood outside the bounds of known histories, and that had no discernable or

discrete architectural features other than a shattered perimeter wall. It took us nearly a month to clear just a portion of the site that first season. Our efforts were concentrated mainly on the site interior rather than the surrounding wall or the areas beyond its outer boundary. This was, afterall, the one part of the site that had not been intensively examined in the previous year. Our efforts were to be rewarded in ways no one had anticipated. In general, we demonstrated that the integrity, or lack of integrity, of surface architecture cannot be used as a measure of site content. Further, that the seemingly ephemeral presence of cultural deposits across the surface of the site is no *fata morgana*; rather, they serve as a kind of barometer indicative of subsurface character. More importantly, however, the first season's crew was integral in the recovery and documentation of a new artifact industry—coral fishhooks. Nothing like it had been recognized or recovered within the archaeological record of Kosrae, the region or the rest of the Pacific. Under their efforts, Safonfok was transformed from a disassembled, disturbed historical site of little significance to a *type site* for a newly identified artifact industry, and a highly significant site of wealth, importance and standing at the time of its occupation.

At the close of our first season, the traditional history of Kosrae was in dire need of reevaluation. Here was a site, a large site, which was continuously occupied from about A.D. 1200 to 1600, a period of great importance in the history of the island. This was a formative period, when large regional centers were vying for power and control over the island's population and resources. Great changes were underway, driven by increasing social and political complexity, shifting land tenure systems, and cultural expectations and societal roles that were systematically and routinely becoming more rigidly defined. Governance of the island was moving from autonomous regional centers toward unification under the dictates of a single power-wielding central place. But as oral histories were recounted, Safonfok did not appear in them. Only Leluh, an unknown but growing center on the eastern coast of the island, played a pivotal role in these narratives. According to these accounts, Leluh's growth and evolution as the central administrative power were unprecedented and proceeded unchecked; there were no credible rivals that could counter its meteoric rise and ultimate victory as the seat of the paramountcy. Until, that is, the results of that first field season at Safonfok.

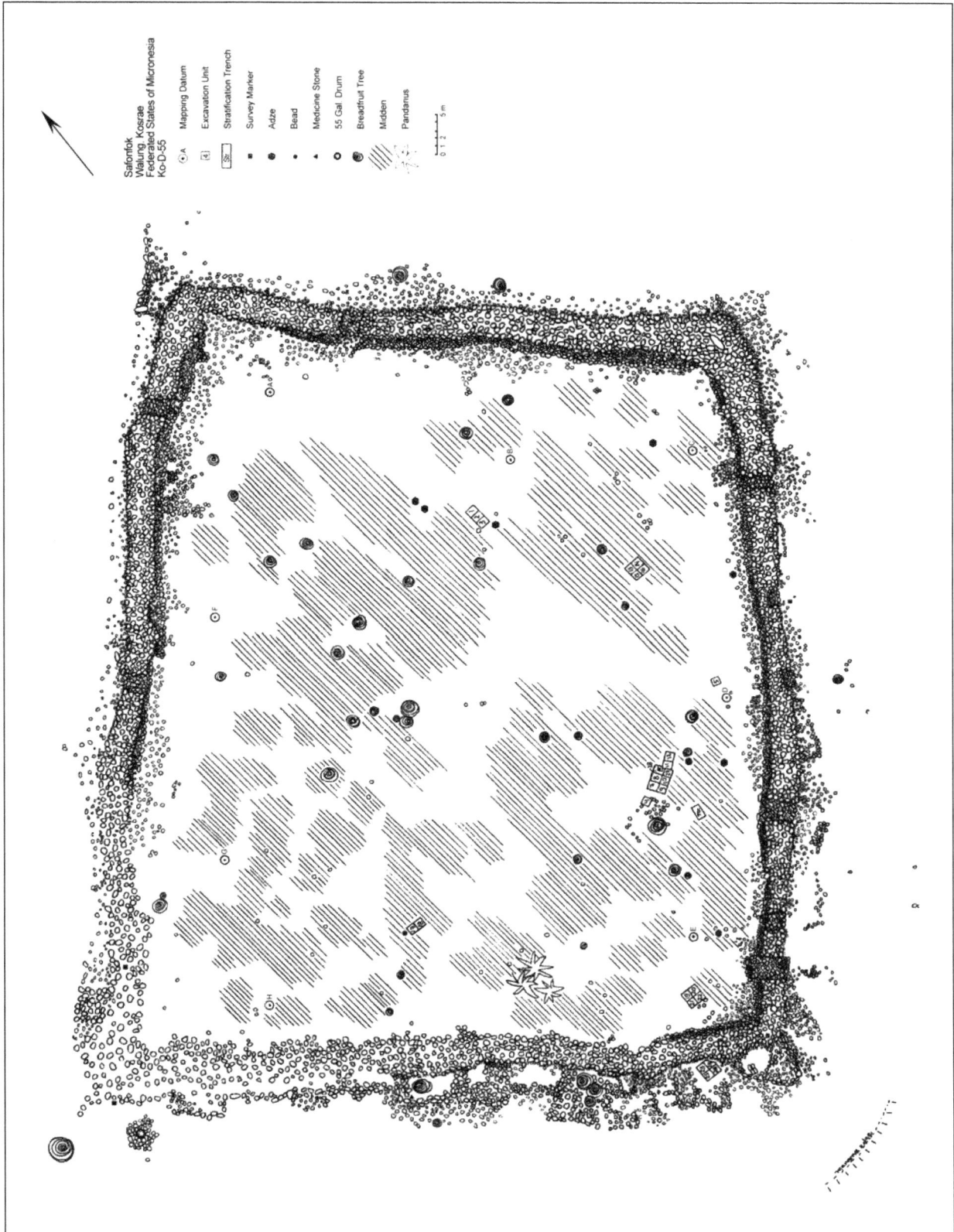

Figure 11. Plan Map of Safonfok.

Too many unresolved questions were raised at the end of that first season; we needed more time at the site to address at least some of these issues. In 2001, we received a second opportunity to return to the site. And, many more details of the site and its content came to light. This was a most productive period. Our efforts this time took on a more holistic approach, with our focus set on the site as a whole. We remapped the entire site and extended our investigation to those areas just beyond the site; we also reexamined the site interior (Figures 11, 12). And, while we knew the site was among the larger sites on the island, its sheer size and extent were made all the more apparent as a result of our more thorough investigation; the site was placed into a category of its own. Here was a site characterized by monumental (albeit collapsed) architecture, with a well planned and designed compound wall displaying an intricate pattern of interlocking coral and basalt boulders, a paved canoe landing that incorporated the natural slope of the adjacent mangrove channel, and a series of spatially discrete enclosures lining the outer edge of one compound wall. The artifact content alone suggested the site supported an elite residence and served as a manufacturing/trading station for tangible goods and medicinal services. Further, both the architecture and cultural content indicated the site was a central location for regional commerce and played host to visiting dignitaries and high-ranking guests. Safonfok too, as it turns out, had the benefit of location; it stood in the heart of the earliest settled region on the island, a position that conferred status, prestige, rank, and privilege.

Our second field season confirmed the significance of the site. Safonfok was elevated to a central administrative power during the formative era in Kosrae's history, at least within its section of the island. Here was a credible opponent to Leluh, and with one advantage Leluh lacked—historical connections to the founding population. This section of the island, the southwest coast, had played host to the first settlers, according to legendary history. Their exact landing location remains veiled by the mists of time, however this general area of the island is said to have supported the longest occupation. It is the place from which status and chiefly position were derived. The standing of chiefs in the island-wide system of prestige and the hierarchy of power was reinforced if they could trace their ancestry to this part of the island through a recitation of genealogies. Such was a demonstration of their deep roots in Kosrae, of their connection to the founding population, and of their assumed connection to the ancestors of the founding population. Even the chiefs of Leluh did their best to demonstrate their long-lived roots to this part of the island. Sites here are considered older than any others on the island; however, until our work at Safonfok, no dates had actually confirmed this status.

After two field seasons of archaeological investigation, Safonfok has emerged as a significant site in the history of Kosrae, one that played a defining role in the shaping of Kosrae culture. Its presence in the archaeological record cannot be ignored and demands a reassessment of the island's traditional history. Or at least a revision of that history, one that can accommodate a large and important administrative center during the formative era of Kosrae's history. Safonfok served as a prominent political center within its region of the island; it played a key role in the economic cycle of the island; it was directly involved in the distribution of wealth and, perhaps, knowledge (e.g., medicine); and, it housed an elite residence that demonstrated differential access to resources. Within the formative era on the island, Safonfok was a power to be reckoned with and likely stood as a formidable foe to the rising, but nascent power at Leluh. The implications of our work at Safonfok also reach far beyond the shores of Kosrae, with the introduction of a newly identified artifact industry within the Pacific archaeological record. It is perhaps fitting to suggest that long-distance interaction patterns as well as settlement histories in this part of the Pacific may also need to be revisited, and possibly revised.

## Safonfok: A Description of the Site

Safonfok is located in a strategic position within the landscape. It rests at a point where the reef meets the shoreline, so that any movement in the lagoon is visible from the northern opening in the reef (some 2 kilometers away) to the point where reef and land merge. It stands alone in this part of the island, bound on the west by the lagoon, on the north by the sandy coastal plain, and on the south and east by the freshwater/mangrove channel that also served as the canoe entrance to the site. The nearest historical sites of some substance, that is site with significant architectural features, are roughly one-half to one kilometer away, to the north and south.

The totality of the ruins at Safonfok consists of the major compound area defined by its surrounding wall and a peripheral zone just beyond the wall incorporating those features that supported the activities within the compound. The term *compound* refers to a series of platforms, foundations, cooking and activity areas clustered within a discrete area surrounded and defined by a rather substantial wall. Such formations are presumed to be the residence of a single, perhaps extended family. However, the sheer size of the Safonfok compound, covering an area of roughly 8,000 square meters, suggests the residents held elite status, with preferential treatment demanded as a result of their assumed political, economic and social standing. The diversity of activities indicated in the archaeological record lends support to the probable function of the site as an important administrative center, at least within its section of the island. In the surrounding peripheral zone, just beyond the wall, there lies a series of significantly

Figure 12. View of Safonfok, from the north (after clearing). Brush piles are stacked throughout the site. This image shows the dearth of internal architecture, e.g. no standing walls.

smaller, conjoined enclosures believed to have been temporary quarters for visiting dignitaries and tradesmen who supported and utilized the administrative center. A paved canoe ramp extends from this outer cluster of rooms into the mangrove channel. A second canoe ramp serves the opposite end of the compound; however, it is more modest in appearance and likely served local (possibly upstream) residents rather than outside visitors.

Extending further north and south from the site, there are fairly dense continuous surface deposits of residential and occupational debris, but no foundations or walls. These deposits are assumed to mark the residential areas for those people who played a substantial role in the domestic support of Safonfok, who served the elite residents in various capacities necessary for a fully functioning center of power. Roughly one kilometer to the south is the walled compound of Koasr, and to the north at about one-half kilometer, there lies another equally dense and very substantial artifact scatter with remnants of stone and coral foundations scattered throughout. But neither of these sites marks the extent of the evidence for occupation on this part of the island; smaller scatters of artifact concentrations, some with remnants of architectural features, continue to be found still farther afield. Our own surveys did not extend beyond the immediate vicinity of Safonfok, nor were they systematic; our efforts and observations of out-laying sites were more fortuitous, the result of encounters as we traveled overland to one or another boat pick-up point or in search of other reported historical sites.

The most prominent feature at Safonfok is its surrounding wall, a sinewy band of coral and basalt boulders that defines a compound which is among the largest on-island. Remnants of the collapsed wall cover an area roughly 3 to 5 meters wide, and spans 100 meters north to south and 80 meters west to east. It is (or rather, was) an unmortared multiple course construction, built with coral boulders, basalt boulders, an occasional boulder-sized basalt column, and an interstitial fill within the wall façade of coral cobbles and pebbles. Structurally, the wall is a complex feature consisting of a double retaining wall supported by a rubble-filled core. It was built in sections, with section division most visible as reinforcements for the series of openings that pass through the wall. Each opening is lined with a façade of undressed basalt and coral uprights; a relatively level, single course pavement extends beyond the limits of the wall into and outside the compound, lining the paths of ingress and egress. One of the openings is flanked at each corner by large coral rounds, suggesting a formal entrance.

A paved walkway lines the outer perimeter of the western (lagoon), northern, and eastern (mangrove) walls of the site; the outer edge of this path is dressed with a single line of coral boulders. Each outer walkway expands substantially, nearly doubling its width, in the vicinity of the wall openings. The outer face of the eastern wall also contains two niches built into the base of the wall; neither are openings, as they do not extend through the wall. On the interior, compound side of the wall, a single course, highly manicured and paved apron adjoins the base of all four walls. Today, the compound wall has collapsed and consists of a sinuous band of tumbled coral and basalt boulders that are continually rearranged by root movement, scavenging activity for land crabs and the general meanderings of pigs and

Figure 13. Specific features associated with the site: a. passage through the north wall, with the intact base alignment on one side, *in situ* pavement, and rubble of opposite side collapsed onto pavement; b. midden concentration common to the site, complete with fire-cracked rock and shell refuse; c. exterior of north wall with outer paved pathway; d. coral boulder alignment with partially buried pavement inside compound.

people as they pass over and through the site in the course of their daily routines (Figure 13).

Inside the compound wall, there are several architectural features, but many are difficult to see. Prior to our

clearing efforts, very little masonry in the form of structural foundations was visible owing to the dense foliage. Jungle covered the entire site, but at least segments of concentrated constructions—the stone wall, for example—could be glimpsed through the ground cover. However, foundations low to the ground or nearly buried, as those encountered inside the compound, remained largely hidden. These foundations consist of single courses of partially buried pavements and alignments. At least one area within the site appears exclusive to the manufacture of *Tridacna* shell adzes, while three cooking/kitchen areas are indicated in dense surface concentrations of a dark, nearly black midden enriched soil (each of these areas are supported by buried earth ovens, or *um* features, observed during excavation). Throughout the site a relatively deep, dark midden of shell, burned stone and artifacts, including coral fishhooks and unique shell beads, extends the full length and width of the compound. It reaches depths of 40 to 80 centimeters below surface and is the most expansive midden deposit reported in the archaeological record of the island.

Just beyond the compound wall lays the peripheral zone. The most significant area within this zone is found on the south side of the compound. Here, a number of conjoining enclosures extend outward from the compound wall. Each enclosure is separated from the adjoining enclosure by a single coral and basalt wall. A stone pavement extends from these dividing walls; however, they appear to be walkways rather than pavements or foundations within the enclosures. At least one of the enclosures appears to be an off-loading/storage room for goods either received or shipped; inside this enclosure is a raised rectangular platform, which is not found in any other enclosure at the site. This particular room is adjacent to a canoe landing described as the principal landing for the site because it consists of a pavement that extends from the southeastern corner of the compound to the shallow slope that descends into the mangrove channel. A second canoe landing appears at the northeastern corner of the site; however, it is not as well defined nor retains any of the substantial paving of the southeastern ramp. One of the other enclosures in this southern complex of enclosures appears to have housed a medicinal specialist. Here, a distinctive basalt grinding stone with a small, deep depression was observed in association with a basalt adze-like tool with a flaked edge intended to process articles such as medicinal plants and plant parts. Within this enclosure, and throughout the compound as well, a number of medicinal plants are growing wild. And, were it not for our own observations that this was the only place, and the only historical site, on this part of the island where such plants were growing, our interpretation of a medicinal specialist housed at Safonfok would make little sense.

The eastern side of the compound, facing the mangrove channel, appears to be the front, or principal side, of the compound. It is here that the formal entryway appears, along with partly buried slope retaining walls and pavements that extend toward the channel, the principal canoe landing, and the adjoining cluster of exterior enclosures.

## Excavations

Our excavations were intended to test and explore all portions of the compound so long as time and the tides allowed. While we did not randomly select excavation areas, as previous experience in excavating site compounds (though much smaller in scale) gave us some idea of what to expect and where, it would be misleading to imply that our excavation strategy followed a precise design. We began with the excavation of a series of stratigraphic pits or trenches to expose the basic geological history of the site, and to provide us with a vertical depositional guide for the ensuing excavations. It would be folly to blindly begin systematic excavations at the site without at least a preliminary idea about what lay below us, about the general stratigraphic sequence upon which the site was formed. Our first two stratigraphic trenches in 1999 exposed mixed deposits that extended for some depth below the surface; our optimism was waning as the specter of a very disturbed site was presented. But, we persevered and excavated one more trench (Figure 14). It exposed an intact stratigraphic sequence, including a thick midden deposit that extended from the surface to a depth of nearly a meter. This was the most extensive archaeological midden deposit reported for the island; just this alone elevated the site in our minds to a new level, one that could potentially tell us something about the range of activities conducted within a large regional center. With renewed enthusiasm, our exploration of the site ensued and we began in earnest to plan the location of each and every excavation unit. Throughout, our strategy was one of opportunism, following up, as circumstances dictated, what looked like fair indications of descriptive and chronological information.

Two seasons of fieldwork have exposed the stratigraphic history of this part of the coastal strand. It is a history that begins in the distant past, with an active (but unoccupied) beach layer (IV) complete with coarse calcareous sand made of comminuted shell and coral. Cobble-sized fragments of unmodified, water-rounded coral are distributed randomly throughout this layer. Over this, a stabilized back-beach deposit (III) formed. Smaller sediment grains dominate a densely packed matrix that likely supported a strand vegetation. The very presence of this back-beach deposit suggests that the active beach was building lagoonward, behind a prograding shoreline. Whether this process reflected a dropping sea level or other natural processes related to the compound motion of wave patterns, currents and the redistribution of sediments remains unresolved. There is no indication of cultural activity within this stabilized beach deposit, with one exception: at the north end of the site, a leveled coral spread appears at the point where the active beach stratum (IV) meets the stabilized beach stratum (III). This coral spread consists of densely packed, well-sorted corals in an arrangement common to man-made pavements observed across the Pacific—with

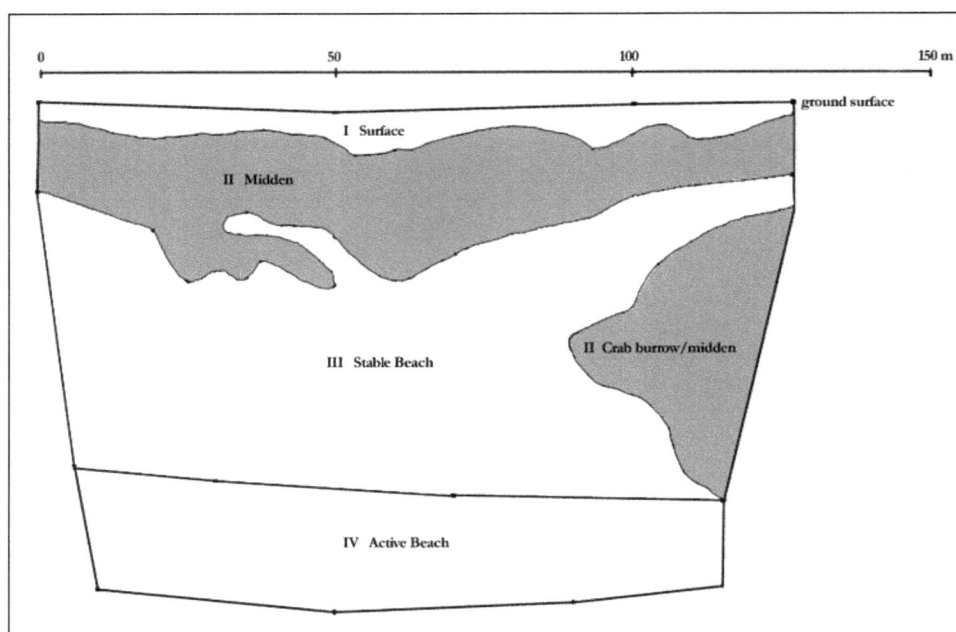

Figure 14. Stratigraphic Trench 3, south face profile. It is this trench that helped define the principle strata within the site.

larger corals concentrated near the top or surface of the feature and smaller corals packed between and below these corals. The fact that this spread does not appear in any other stratigraphic profile across the site raises questions about its origin, and will require further and more intensive examination. Does the coral spread represent the earlier presence of people on this part of the coastal plain, within the site area? Does it represent an isolated tidal surge event that inundated only one part of the site area and no other? Are there other causal explanations that could account for this anomalous feature?

The principal cultural stratum (II), a dark almost black midden, overlays the stabilized beach deposit. It stands in sharp contrast to the lighter colored, yellowish underlying strata, although the nature of the sediments—sands—encourages mixing at the transition point. Within Layer II proper, evidence for occupation is densely distributed and contains the full range of artifacts and cultural materials representative of the diverse activities that occurred within the site at the time of occupation. Artifacts recovered throughout this layer include coral fishhooks, shell beads and coral tools; the full range of debitage associated with the manufacture of both fishhooks and beads; a shell fishhook; shell adzes and adze fragments; shell and coral drills; basalt knife fragments and flakes; a basalt sledge-hammer; a medicine processing tool; shell hinges used in the adze manufacturing process; fire-cracked rock and coral; charcoal; and midden (subsistence) remains. Architectural features encountered include several *um*, or

earth ovens, the suggestion of the presence of *um* in the form of concentrated fire-cracked rock rack-outs, and a pavement of coral boulders with an interstitial fill of coral spread. The *um* are characterized by rounded depressions that extend from the midden layer into the underlying stabilized beach layer. They contain bands of charcoal and ash, as well as burnt coral, shell and rock.

The uppermost stratigraphic layer (I), visible across the entire site, is the layer of abandonment. It consists of the upper portion of Layer II, coupled with thin lenses of aerially deposited sands as well as sand lenses that appear to be the result of storm surges. Crab burrows are common, with many of the burrows extending into the underlying strata; pig damage is also evident in the guise of rutted depressions and displaced deadfall, cobbles and other features that harbor tasty, sought-after treats; and stratigraphic mixing appears in those areas directly affected by crabs, pigs and even the movement of tree roots and spread of vegetation.

A total of 28 units were laid out and excavated across the site; six units during our first field season, the remaining 22 during our second. Concurrent with the excavations, surface surveys and mapping activities produced a detailed record of surface features and artifact concentrations, the full extent of the compound wall including its several openings, the series of enclosures appended to the outer edge of the compound wall, and the main and ancillary canoe landings. The first series of excavation units (Units 1 to 6) were scattered throughout the site, with their locations based on the presence and density of artifacts on the site surface. In 2001, excavation units were distributed throughout seven excavation blocks or unit clusters (Table 1), the first of which were placed initially in the most artifact rich areas of 1999; the remainder were placed in areas where surface deposits and the cast-out debris of crab burrows suggested the presence of concentrated buried cultural deposits.

Table 1. 2001 Excavation Blocks and Units.

| Block | Dimensions (m) | Orientation (mag. N) | Unit Numbers |
|---|---|---|---|
| I | 2-x-2 | 326° | 7, 8, 9, 10 |
| II | 1-x-2 | 320° | 11, 12 |
| III | 2-x-2 | 0° | 13, 14, 15, 16 |
| IV | 1-x-2 | 0° | 17, 18 |
| V | 2-x-2 | 0° | 19, 20, 21, 22 |
| VI | 2-x-2 | 0° | 23, 24, 25, 26 |
| VII | 2-x-1.2* | 326° | 27, 28 |

* Encompasses the unexcavated area between Blocks I and II.

The 1999 Units 1, 2 and 3 were contiguous, creating essentially a systematically excavated trench one meter wide by three meters long. It was placed in an area where surface scatters contained *Tridacna* shell adzes and adze manufacturing debris, along with midden (food shell), and fire-cracked rock. The excavation exposed the same stratigraphic sequence observed throughout the site, but also displayed much disturbance from crab burrows that mixed sediments. One *um* was also observed in the excavation; it consisted of charcoal infused sediments that contained burned shell and bone. It was sampled specifically for radiocarbon dating.

Unit 4 was placed directly adjacent to the only relatively intact structural foundation observed within the site interior. This was a single alignment of coral boulders that adjoined a small coral pavement extending outward from the alignment. Crabs had made their presence known in the form of borrows that upended and displaced some of the corals in the alignment; in the center of the enclosure, there was a very large breadfruit tree with roots that also distorted the alignment. This unit in particular was something of a bellwether; it represented the beginning of the transformation of Safonfok into something more than just a large compound. The first of what was to be many coral fishhooks was recovered from this unit, along with the debris from the manufacturing of such hooks. Other cultural materials that were to become commonplace in our recovery efforts were also observed here: subsistence remains, fragments of coral and shell tools, charcoal, fire-cracked rock and coral, shell adze debitage,

the remains from the manufacture of shell beads, and the remains of an occasional stone flake fragment.

Within five meters from Unit 4, a thick nearly black midden covered the ground surface. We hypothesized that this was a kitchen area, perhaps associated with the structure by which we had been excavating. The thickest, darkest part of the surface scatter was dominated by a large tree and various shrubs. There were a lot of roots visible throughout the area. But, we managed to find a small area between roots that offered real possibilities for a brief window into the buried deposits. This became our Unit 6, which we placed in the middle of a thick deposit of food remains and fire-cracked rock. The unit produced a wide range of coral fishhooks and the debris from their manufacture, as well as a unique diamond-shaped bead (such a bead had never been reported for the island), the debris from bead manufacture, food remains (shell and bone), charcoal, fire cracked rock, and large coral tools unlike any that had been recovered on the island. The coral tools were unique in that they were made from a soft, but coarsely textured coral that retained the pressure imprints of the hand that had gripped them during their use. At least one of the tools exhibited a broad flat surface on one of its sides, and looked much like a tool that might be used in wood working, perhaps in the construction of canoes.

The final unit of the 1999 field season, Unit 5, was located at a point roughly between Units 1-2-3 and Units 4-6, in the only part of the site that was littered with *Tridacna* fragments, an area we referred to as the adze workshop. We recovered no *Tridacna* adzes in this area, only the telltale debris of their manufacture. Within the unit, an abbreviated stratigraphic sequence was observed. All the strata visible across the site were present in the same order of their appearance, but Layers I and II, the uppermost layer and the principal cultural deposit, were relatively shallow. Our recovery too was rather light, consisting primarily of *Tridacna* fragments and little else. Other than the *Tridacna* fragments, little other cultural debris was visible on the surface in this part of the site, which reinforced our observations that surface deposits reflected the content of buried deposits.

During the 2001 field season, Blocks I, II, and VII were placed within the span between Units 4 and 6; in fact, Block VII actually encompassed Unit 6. The culturally rich deposits encountered in 1999 prompted this more intensive and extensive excavation. Initially, Blocks I and II were to remain discrete and separate excavations; however, near the end of the field season we systematically removed the ground between these two Blocks. This interloping area became Block VII, and proved to be as rich or even richer in cultural materials than the two flanking Blocks I and II. Across this combined three-block excavation, the cultural stratum, Layer II, was thicker and more extensive than we had expected (Figure 15). Several *um* were encountered,

Figure 15. Block I, showing midden layer atop the stable, back-beach deposit. Scale points toward magnetic north.

along with their associated rake-outs of fire-cracked rock. A wide variety of artifacts were recovered throughout this area, from coral fishhooks to several different kinds and shapes of shell beads, to a shell fishhook that is a rarity in archaeological deposits on Kosrae, to still more coral tools much like those recovered in 1999, as well as shell adzes (*Tridacna* and *Terebra*), the debris from shell and coral manufacturing industries, and food debris (shell and bone). This was, by all appearances, a working area for the former occupants of the site. The image burned into our minds during the excavation was one of various sorts of craftsmen congregated around the kitchen fires, talking story, working on their respective crafts, fashioning coral and shell fishhooks, shell beads, other utilitarian or ornamental objects, or perhaps even working on a canoe stationed nearby.

Block III was placed in the northeastern quadrant of the site, in an area that was excessively brushy. It took a lot of effort to clear this portion of the site, but in the end we were rewarded (Figure 16). The surface was littered with food remains (shell mainly) and fire-cracked rock brought up by the crabs. This alone suggested another food processing area that would likely contain an *um* or perhaps several *um*. We were not disappointed. The excavations exposed several *um*, one of which contained several large pieces of charcoal that would be useful as samples for identification as well as radiocarbon dating. One of the excavation units within the Block continued to a point well into the lowest stratigraphic layer in the sequence common to the rest of the site, Layer IV. Even without this deeper excavation, Block III exposed that enigmatic coral spread at the point where Layer IV meets Layer III. It is a compact layer of cobble-sized coral

fragments, distributed in an even, well-sorted and relatively thin leveled band reminiscent of a pavement. But is it? Sediments from the stratigraphic layers above and below this anomalous feature break away from it, leaving it intact and in place; a material and physical comment to the compact nature of the pavement, perhaps even silent testimony to its compactness and its likely history as a planned piece of architecture rather than an isolated tidal event.

Excavation Block IV was disappointing. On the surface beads, bead blanks and bead-making shells were observed. But below the surface, stratigraphic mixing was quite evident. The mixing extended through the entire stratigraphic sequence, from the surface to the basal active beach layer. It is likely both pigs and crabs were the principal agents of the mixing. Little cultural material was recovered.

Block V was placed in the southern corner of the site, adjacent to a partial alignment of coral boulders and just across the wall from the series of outer enclosures. An *um* was encountered as well as food shell and bone, some of which looked like turtle bone, and bone that looked surprisingly human. No burials were encountered, however. The presence of turtle bone suggests the remnants of a meal(s) for high status or elite figures, as this was a traditionally restricted food. Beyond this, recovery included the general assortment of cultural material that had by now become routine and expected: coral fishhooks and debitage, bead-making shell, charcoal, a basalt knife fragment (the conjoining piece of this knife was located outside the compound walls, just beyond the outer enclosures), and fire-cracked rock.

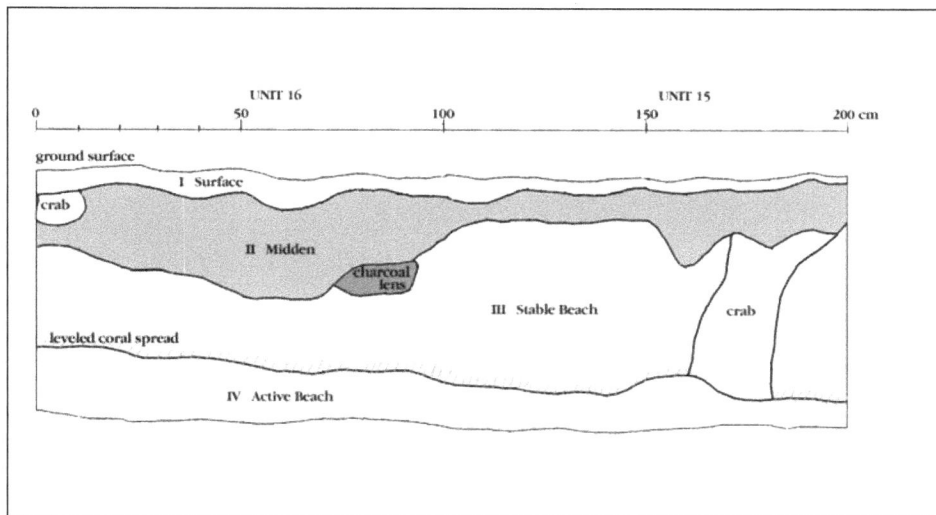

Figure 16. Block III, Unit 16 south wall showing coral spread/pavement at base of profile in photograph; Units 16-15 south wall profile above.

Block VI was the only excavation placed outside the compound, in the area peripheral to the site. It was placed within one of the enclosures adjacent to the southern compound wall (Figure 17). Our intent was to determine the physical, structural appearance of these enclosures, followed by their use or uses. To what extent had these enclosures been used as domestic quarters, quarters for visiting dignitaries, tradesmen, or other purposes? Closely related to this question was one of function. Were these permanently inhabited, temporarily inhabited, or did they serve as a sort of quarantine quarters? And, what was the period of use? Did they come later in the occupational sequence of the compound, or had they been in concurrent use with the site's activities? The results of our excavations need some additional evaluation and rumination, but we did find that there was a prepared floor within the enclosure. It consisted of a coral spread composed of pebble-sized fragments commingled with the local sandy sediments. A pattern of boulders was evident within the enclosure as

well, aligned in a somewhat rectangular pattern; its function remains unresolved for the present.

## Oral History

The collection of oral histories related to Safonfok has proven to be a rather difficult task. Few residents of Walung recognized the site as an historic place, and only two informants—a mother and her son—were able to provide any information. According to both, the site is very old and had high walls at one time; this is what they had heard, they said, and they could add nothing more. Otherwise, oral histories attached to the site refer to a more recent time, long after abandonment. It is during the active occupation of the nearby Mwot Mission School and construction of the first elementary school in Walung that stories surrounding the site seem to concentrate. Children from the Mission School, for example, are blamed for the tumbled-down state of the wall. They used to hunt for land crabs within the rock and rubble of the walls, raking these structures apart in the search for these tasty little beasties. The site ruins provided excellent habitat for land crabs, and those in search of these elusive animals would frequently visit the area in the hope of capturing several at a time. Little concern was given for the integrity and stability of these old walls in the wake of the hunt.

Safonfok played a central role in another story relating events that took place during the initial years of the Mission. A family from the Marshall Islands, the story goes, was shipwrecked on Kosrae. They had been blow off-course during their sojourn between Likieup and Ebon. They landed on the southern coast of Kosrae and made the best of their situation in a new place, not knowing where or in what direction their own islands lay. At one point, one of the Marshallese became very ill, so the family, having heard of a doctor at the Mission, sent a

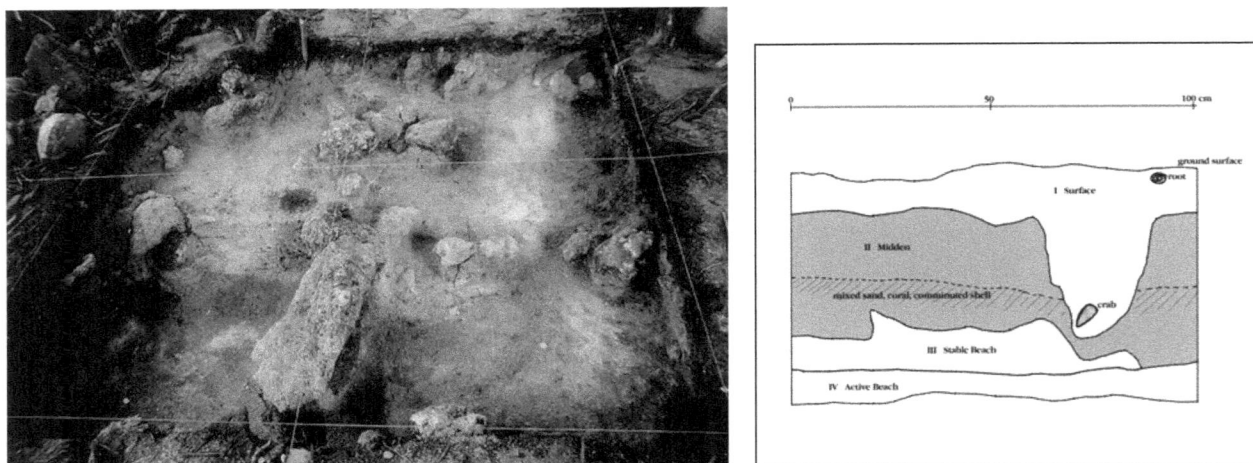

Figure 17. Block VI, planview photograph of block showing architectural features resting on a prepared coral floor. Crushed coral pavement visible in lower half of block. Stratigraphic profile of Unit 23 (lower left corner in photograph) north wall showing vertical location of prepared coral floor (noted as 'mixed sand, coral, comminuted shell').

smal contingent of their members in search of medical assistance. The missionaries suggested the entire family move closer to the Mission in order to better treat their ailing member. So, the family took up residence in the abandoned historic site of Koasr, on the southwest coast; this was closer to the Mission than their own settlement, but still some distance from the Mission. After several visits to the Mission, the missionaries convinced the Marshallese family to move still closer, so the family moved into Safonfok. The walls of the compound were still, apparently, standing, as this was before the Mission children tore them down. It was here the Marshallese family remained for several years. What modifications they made to the site during their residence remain unknown.

When the first public elementary school was constructed in Walung during the Trust Territory Time, materials for its foundation were mined from the rubble of the Safonfok wall, according to our informants. In particular, the western corner of the Safonfok wall seems to have received the brunt of this 'borrowing,' as the coral and basalt boulders within this portion are sparsely distributed across and beyond the area that once formed the wall foundation. Importing building materials to this part of Kosrae is not only expensive, but fraught with innumerable difficulties owing to the timing of tides and the perils of small boat travel. So, when a ready-made source of building materials is already present in the guise of rubble piles at a site to which no historical ties seem to exist, places like Safonfok become a principal source of building stone. The walls of Safonfok were not only mined for construction of the elementary school foundation, but also for the foundations of other structures within Walung.

# V. MATERIAL CULTURE ANALYSES

Archaeological research is not conducted in a vacuum, nor is it confined to fieldwork alone. The second necessary and vitally important stage in any archaeological investigation is the work undertaken in the laboratory—analysis of recovered artifacts and scientific samples. This process usually begins in the field, with a limited effort engaged to begin the raw sorting of artifacts and scientific samples—isolating charcoal fragments from each sample, identifying the range of formal artifact types present, providing a rough mental map of what was collected in which part of the site. It is at this stage, the first inklings of laboratory analysis, as well as the more in-depth studies of recovered materials, that the past begins to unfold systematically, in a level of detail generally not visible or accessible during the heat of fieldwork. This is the time when research questions are addressed and refined, when the functions of features are disclosed, when chronologies are created, tested, verified and defined, and when the activities conducted within the confines of a site emerge from the fog of the past and are subjected to interpretation with greater clarity.

The following pages describe the results of laboratory analysis on the cultural materials recovered during fieldwork. It is divided into two sections: *Material Culture* and *Specialized Analyses*. The former is a summary of artifacts and tangible remains by formal type; the latter summarizes the evidence of human activity primarily in the form of radiocarbon dates and chronologies.

## Material Culture

The range of artifacts recovered over the course of fieldwork include adzes, beads, fishhooks, tools used in the construction of canoes and in the reduction of raw materials, the full complement of debris from the reduction process, and a variety of other tools, implements and articles. Notably absent from the artifact assemblage are historic era artifacts and materials—none were observed nor collected over the course of archaeological investigations. Of the traditional era assemblage, coral fishhooks turned out to be one of the more ubiquitous artifacts recovered from the site, as well as the harbinger for an elevated status of Safonfok (Figure 18). The coral fishhooks are the first examples of their kind in the Pacific, with the exception of a 19th century reference (albeit without physical specimens) to

their antiquity in Tuvalu (Beasley 1928, Hedley 1896). Their presence at Safonfok has transformed the site into a *type site* or *reference site* for coral fishhooks, and provided the mechanism for their inclusion in the archaeological assemblages of Kosrae and the region. Other artifacts recovered from Safonfok include a basalt knife, diamond-shaped and teardrop-shaped shell beads, coral abraders complete with impression imprints from the hand that gripped them, and a basalt sledge-hammer found in association with large *Tridacna* shells in the process of being reduced. Like the coral fishhooks, all these artifacts are fabricated using traditional manufacturing techniques and locally available raw materials.

The following pages describe the recovered artifacts by basic formal category.

### Fishhooks and Fishing Technology

In the history of mechanical apparatus, fishhooks are very ancient and ubiquitous, depending on where you are in the world (Anell 1955, Beasley 1928, Emory, Bonk and Sinoto 1959). They occur in artifact assemblages across the Pacific, including Kosrae. However, until our work at Safonfok, fishhooks from archaeological contexts on-island were rare and consisted of a single one-piece, simple pearl shell fishhook recovered in 1910 by Hambruch (Sarfert 1919, Yawata 1930, Cordy 1993) and 17 pearl shell lures recovered by Cordy during his 1980-81 fieldwork (Cordy 1993). All these fishhooks were recovered from the Leluh compounds, where their associations with elite households and burial chambers impressed Hambruch, Yawata and Cordy as ornaments rather than more practical, functional implements. At Safonfok, a single shell fishhook fragment and a whole series of coral fishhooks (a new artifact type for Kosrae and the region) were recovered, along with the manufacturing debris associated with the coral fishhook industry (Figures 19, 20). Other fishing related implements recovered from the site include coral net or line sinkers and a coral toggle, a common component of compound/composite fishhooks. The sheer quantity of fishing related technology—from debris to finished implements—recovered throughout the site deposit attest to the economic importance of the sea and its products for the residents of Safonfok. Their associations too with myriad household debris and midden deposits strongly suggest their use as functional, practical apparatus rather than ornamental baubles, amulets or other non-functional devices.

Figure 18. This is the first coral fishhook recovered from Safonfok. It is no more than 3 cm long, yet served as the herald for a whole new type of artifact industry recovered throughout the site.

Within the overall category of fishhooks as artifacts, there are many different kinds; yet they all tend to fall into three basic categories: single hooks, two-piece hooks (the latter are often referred to as compound hooks, but are actually two pieces of a single hook), and compound hooks (like bonito and octopus lures; Emory, Bonk and Sinoto 1959). Among these, there are hooks that penetrate the mouth or throat of a fish, where the points are concealed by bait; there are penetrative hooks where no bait is used, but the hook is fashioned from bright materials and rotates in the water like a spinner or lure; and, there are still other hooks that hold bait in such a way that the fish cannot suck it off but most swallow the hook and bait together. Each is tailored to the type of fish to be caught and its propensity for taking bait whole or in part, or simply its attraction toward bright shining objects.

Across the Pacific, fishhooks are found in various states of completion. Mostly, though, they are fragmented, broken and damaged. By comparison, very few complete hooks are ever recovered. The kinds of fishhooks most often encountered include an early form described as a U-shaped, or jabbing hook which has a straight shank and straight (or slightly incurved) point, a knobbed or notched head at the top of the shank for the line attachment and snood, and no barbs. Another common form is the gorge, also considered among the earliest, but it has not been demonstrated to be any earlier than the jabbing hook (Anell 1955). The gorge is generally straight to V-shaped, pointed at both ends, with the line tied in the center; it functions in roughly similar fashion to the jabbing hook, except that it is generally swallowed along with the bait. There are also rotating hooks, where either the point or shank or both are mostly curved, and circular hooks in which both shank and point are curved to form a somewhat off-center circle; some of these will be barbed, some not. All of these forms are classified as single hooks. Two-piece fishhooks include various

shapes of both shanks and points; compound hooks are composites that include various shapes of shanks and points, along with the addition of other elements used to produce the lure.

Whether a single, two-piece or compound hook, there is always some variation in the production and final product, depending on materials used and the fisherman's intended prey and catch strategy (Johannes 1981). Materials govern both the size and type of hook created. There are hooks made from wood, bone (human, whale, dog, moa, animal), teeth (dog), tusk (pig), shell (Trochus, abalone, pearl), turtle shell, thorns, insect parts, stone (green stone, basalt), stalactite, ivory, coconut shell, and iron (Anell 1955, Beasley 1928, Emory, Bonk and Sinoto 1959, Maude and Lampert 1967). There are hooks with barbs, without barbs, curved, and straight. And all are tied with cordage, although line attachments may differ; they may consist of a knob, a notch or a simple but slight groove.

But fishhooks made from coral? In all the reports on fishhooks in the Pacific, the only mention of coral is as a material most often reserved for tools, files, abraders, and sinkers. Coral as a material for fishhooks appears only in references by Hedley (1896) and Beasley (1928). In his account of Funafuti Atoll, Tuvalu, Hedley (1896) states, "...the matou tifa [large somewhat ringed hooks] were formerly carved out of pearl shell or hard coral, but these have passed out of use." Some thirty years later, Beasley presented a summary of fishhooks from the Ellice (Tuvalu) Group, essentially reiterating Hedley:

> From this Group comes what must surely be one of the earliest types of primitive hooks to be found anywhere in the Pacific. Others, it is true, show cruder forms or less skillful workmanship, but none, I venture to think, offer less practicable outlines combined with unsuitability of material. It is recorded that in very early times hooks were ground out of coral, but to my knowledge no specimen of such a hook exists at the present day [Beasley 1928: 25].

Coral as Material. Coral as a raw material is highly resilient and hardens when exposed to air. It is a living organism that grows in many different shapes and sizes, and ultimately resembles various types of terrestrial plants. Some look like lettuce or mushrooms, cauliflower, or even bushes. For many years, if not centuries, it was assumed coral was a plant until the discovery that it was composed of polyps, tiny animals with just two layers of cells that build a skeleton from calcium extracted from the sea (Hedley 1896). Coral polyps reproduce by creating identical copies of themselves, which then remain attached to the parent as they grow. Eventually the newly reproduced copies bud and the cycle begins anew. This newly formed colony of

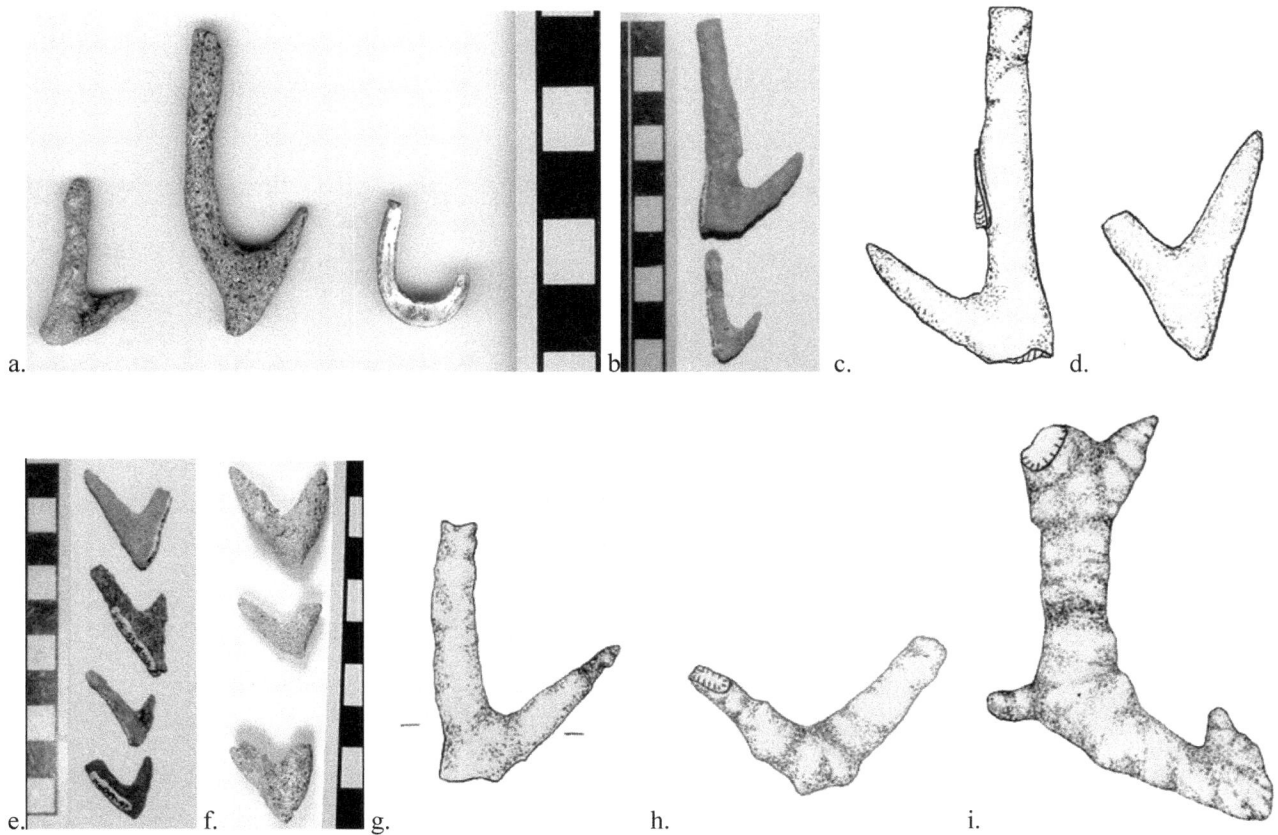

Figure 19. Fishhooks: a. two coral fishhooks and the only shell fishhook (fragmentary) to be recovered from the site; b. two additional coral fishhooks; c. coral fishhook illustrated in (b) and showing line attachment; d. fishhook fragment, missing point (32.4 x 18.9 x 5.8 mm); e. more coral fishhook fragments; f. three gorges; g. coral fishhook recovered from Kosrae Village Resort, damaged point that suggests use as a drill of sorts (50.2 x 34.3 x 9.7 mm); h. gorge recovered from Kosrae Village Resort (22.5 x 35.9 x 6.7 mm); i. shank portion of a two-piece coral fishhook recovered from Kosrae Village Resort, this is the only two-piece fishhook fragment recovered on-island (95 x 65.3 x 16.8 mm).

polyps continues to spawn, bud and grow; ultimately, the plant-like form of coral emerges (Young 1999).

In some sense, this cluster of organisms is more closely related than a family because the polyps remain attached to each other and have identical genetic endowments. As budding proceeds and the colony builds, polyps live side by side, constructing the bony structure characteristic of the particular species to which they belong. Some colonies consist of tightly spaced polyps, in others polyps are widely spaced and surrounded by a broad foundation of limestone. Marine conditions too affect certain shapes in coral colonies. The rough waters of the open ocean are more suited to coral heads of massive compact shapes that can survive the pounding of the sea, whereas, in quiet protected waters, the more delicate branching forms thrive (Hedley 1896, Young 1999). Within the archaeological inventory of Safonfok, the fishhooks and fishhook debris are all branching corals, which likely came directly from the more sheltered waters of the lagoon. The tools, however, are made from a variety of

different corals, from lobed, globular forms to branching corals (these tools are discussed below).

Manufacturing Technology. The production of shell fishhooks is well-known in the Pacific ethnographic and archaeological literature. The whole process begins with the formation of a roughed-out tab, which represents the first stage in the process of creating a fishhook (Sinoto 1979). A tab, or subrectangular shaped fragment, is cut to the approximate size of the intended fishhook. From this point, a series of holes are drilled into the approximate center and off-center of the tab to begin the process of fashioning the inner curve and bend of the hook. The tab itself is also modified, with both the edges and the shank and bend segments starting to take shape. Hook blanks are the final stage before actual finishing work, and involve the removal of excess material to form the inner edges of the hook that create the distinctive bend separating point from shank. The shell fishhook fragment recovered from Safonfok retains enough attributes to classify it as a single, jabbing hook fashioned in this manner.

The manufacture of coral fishhooks takes a slightly different course than shell. The mechanics, mode and technology used in the fashioning of coral fishhooks is mostly visible in the debitage, and to some extent in the fishhooks themselves. In some sense, each and every artifact carries its own blueprint, which allows us to envision how it was used as well as how it was made (Bronowski 1978). With coral, the process is a little more complicated. Manufacturing marks are not readily visible owing to the surface characteristics of the coral. At best, one can determine if the surface has been ground smooth and if branches have been cropped to terminate in blunted, flattened ends. As for the fishhooks themselves, they have certainly been ground and shaped; the surfaces are smooth, the points pointed, line attachments carved into the shank, the heads and bends blunted or even slightly rounded. But, not visible on the artifact surfaces are the residues, marks and cuts from the implement(s) used to shape the fishhook. At best, one can say that the fishhook-shaping toolkit consisted of coral files, small sized abraders, and perhaps shell implements for cutting as well as cropping extra branches and possibly for creating grooves for line attachments.

The Safonfok assemblage consists of debitage, blanks, performs, and completed hooks (sometimes whole, mostly fragmented). The finished hooks fall into two main categories—jabbing hooks and gorges, both single hook types. The first coral fishhook recovered from Safonfok—the hook that captured our attention and defied any attempts to classify it as anything other than a new artifact type—was a very simple single jabbing hook. It consisted of a stem and branch configuration, with the branch filed to a point, the bend finished by grinding and rounding, the shank smoothed and rounded, and a notched line attachment carved into the head of the shank. It had, in other words, all the basic features of a fishhook, yet it was coral—not shell, not bone, not any of the other materials associated with hook manufacture. As digging continued that first field season, more fishhooks, fishhook fragments and debitage from the manufacturing process showed up in the screens. The full complement of both jabbing hooks and gorges began to accumulate, with the inventory growing still further through the second field season. There were, however, no two piece or compound hooks in the assemblage. But that doesn't mean they weren't present in the archaeological assemblage of the island.

Nearly four years later, in 2003, the shank portion of a two-piece fishhook would be recovered from the grounds of the Kosrae Village Resort, on the east coast of Kosrae (Figure 19g-i). The shank is smoothed, with all the roughened heads of the coral polyps ground flat and smooth, all ancillary branches removed and filed flush into the shank, and while no line attachments have been cut into this implement, the coral itself betrays a series of line attachments pressed (or compressed) into the body of the shank. The only attribute missing from this implement is a point. However, the overall shape of the shank/bend/point base confirms the fact that the original production plan did not include a point; that was to be a separate piece added onto the shank and tied in place by a webbing of lines.

The debitage observed and collected throughout the Safonfok deposit appears to be from the initial preparation of selected branching coral fragments, with pieces that have been cast aside as excess or unusable. Fragments of upper terminal twigs commingle with segments of stems and branches in multiple planes with each ending in a blunted cut.

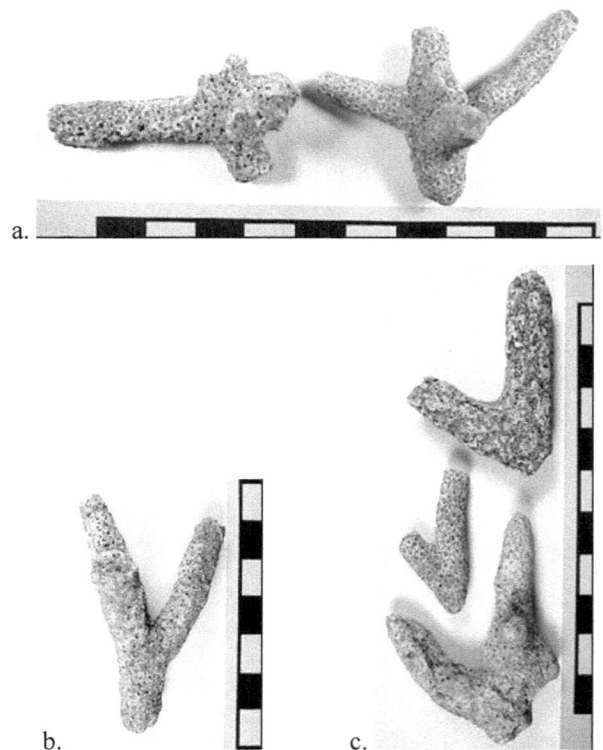

Figure 20. Fishhook production debitage: a. discarded by-projects from the manufacturing process; b. fishhook blank; c. performs.

Blanks are segments of branching coral with just one branch extending from the stem, usually at an angle ranging from 40 to 80 degrees. Additional branches and branchlets have been cropped close to the stem, but are not yet flush against the shank, as in a preform. Excess material is often present, but will eventually be removed as the process of actually shaping the hook continues.

The next category, preforms, consists of nearly completed fishhooks. All specimens display some form of shaping. Excess branches and branchlets have been ground nearly flush to the stem surface; the overall surface itself is smoothed, with the spiky terminus of the polyps removed; points are in the process of being ground into shape; the bend is smoothed or nearly rounded, and the shank is smoothed with the head rounded and line attachment shaped.

The final category is that of complete or finished hooks. So far, Safonfok has remitted two types of finished hooks during excavations and in laboratory analysis. Both are simple, single piece hooks: the jabbing hook and the gorge.

Other Fishing Related Implements. This category includes net or line sinkers made from coral, as well as apparatus that appear to have served as toggles, components in compound or composite fishhooks (Figure 21). The sinkers are partially ground and generally lobed to bell-shape, with indented line impressions confined to a waisted hafting zone and/or terminal knob. They are simple implements, perhaps even somewhat crude in execution as they do not require any degree of complex manufacturing techniques.

Toggles, on the other hand, are not particularly complex but they do require more sophistication in their binding, fitting and handling. The possible toggles recovered from Safonfok retain a web of indented line impressions, with some grinding evident to smooth roughened, angular surfaces (but not to produce a fine finish across the surfaces of these items). Such implements are indicative of compound/composite fishhooks and are frequently used to assist in lashing together various elements needed for a completed hook (e.g., Emory, Bonk and Sinoto 1959). Once assembled, these hooks would have been used to capture selected prey, possibly dwelling in the deep waters outside the reef.

## Adzes, Sledge-Hammers and the Manufacturing Process

Eleven shell adzes (whole, fragmentary, preforms, and blanks) were recovered during both surface surveys and excavations across Safonfok. *Tridacna* and *Terebra* were the principal shells of choice, with at least one adze made from *Hippopus*. The presence of *Tridacna* flakes in both surface and subsurface contexts, along with reduction debris that included a hefty basalt sledge-hammer used in reducing *Tridacna* valves, suggests that *Tridacna* adzes, preforms and blanks were produced on-site. Whether the same can be said of the *Terebra* and *Hippopus* adzes is only speculative at this point, although by extension one could argue that their manufacture and distribution were as equally controlled as *Tridacna* adzes.

Adzes have a wide distribution across the Pacific and often comprise the largest recognizable formal implement in archaeological assemblages where little or no pottery exists. They are, in effect, *de facto* regional chronological and cultural markers, serving much the same purpose as well sequenced pottery or projectile points, wherein their very presence at a site can telegraph

both cultural affiliation and relative age. With the prospects of defining local and regional culture histories in mind, numerous typologies and classificatory strategies have been proposed for Pacific adzes (Green 1974, Duff 1970, Spoehr 1957, Kirch and Yen 1982, Craib 1977, Osborne 1966, 1979). Most of the attention has focused on stone adzes, however, which generally excludes low island cultures and other islands dependent on marine resources for raw materials. Shell adzes have often been perceived as unkempt orphans in these typologies because they display such highly variable shapes and cutting edges heavily influenced by the shell body, mass and shape.

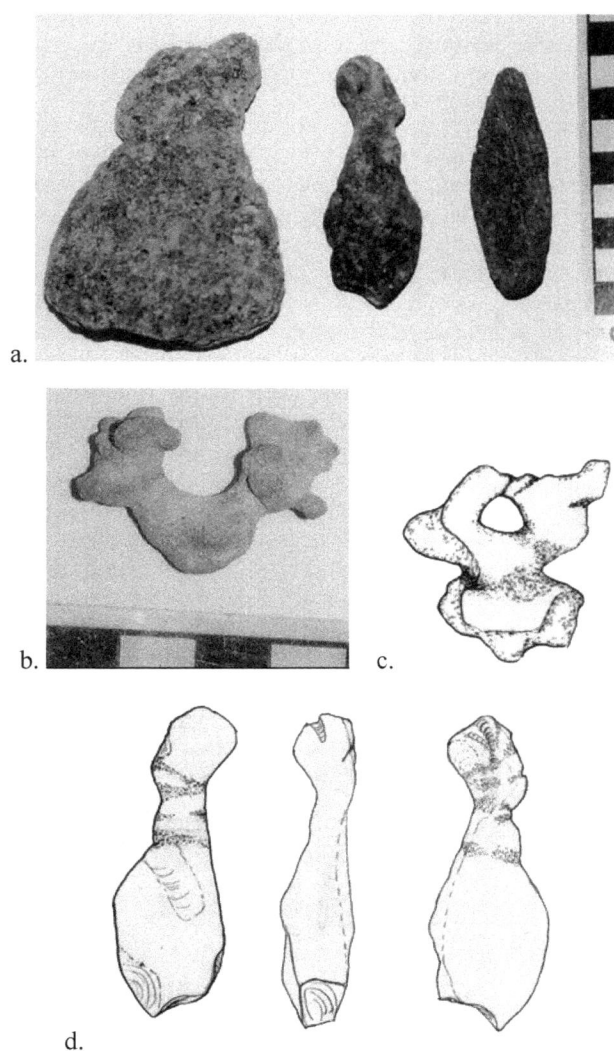

Figure 21. Fishing-related implements: a. coral sinkers or net weights an abrader (discussed below); b.,c. coral toggles; d. coral sinker or net weight (in the center of photograph a), showing line attachment marks.

47

Among the first to promote a comprehensive application of a shell adze typology were Kirch and Yen (1982). Their classificatory scheme for adzes from Tikopia addresses the discrepancy in suitable typologies for shell adzes, as well as the wide range of variability seen in such collections. Although their analytical system was developed primarily for Tikopia and, as they have stated, not for application on a region-wide basis, for comparative purposes they assigned various collections from other western Pacific islands to the types developed under their procedures. Kirch and Yen's typology (with local variations) has been used by others working in the region (Reeve 1989, Favreau 1993, 1995, Beardsley 1994, 1996, 1997a), and is quickly becoming a standard measure for comparison. Their basic attributes and resultant types provide a useful guide for analysis, and have been adopted here with, of course, the necessary adjustments and modifications to meet local conditions.

In general, adzes are wood-working tools. A taxonomic description might define them something like this: cutting, chopping, or gouging implements with a single ground bevel on the working edge (at the bit or distal end) and hafted (at the poll, rear or proximal end) at a right angle to a handle. Other, similarly fashioned implements such as chisels (long narrow implements with an asymmetrical bevel that may or may not have been hafted to a handle) are also included in this category of artifact. Both stone and shell are used as the raw materials for adze manufacture, with a fine grained basalt frequently the material of choice when and where available. Shells used in the manufacture of adzes tend to be structurally dense and include *Tridacna maxima*, *T. gigas*, *T. squamosa*, *T. crocea*, sometimes *Hippopus hippopus*, *Lambis lambis*, *Cassis cornuta*, *C. rufa*, *Conus leopardus*, and still other shells such as *Cyprae cassis*, *Terebra* and *Mitra*. By far, however, *Tridacna* is the most common material of choice, and most likely *T. maxima*, although it is often difficult to determine the species level owing to the manufacturing process, which tends to erase all diagnostic features used to identify species (Moir 1986-87, Kirch and Yen 1982).

Manufacturing Process. Fabrication of an adze begins with selection of the shell to be reduced. With *Tridacna*, three areas of the shell were used—the hinge, dorsal or valve region, and margin of the valve; for other shell types, such as *Cassis*, the lip and whorl or body were used, and for shells like *Terebra*, the entire shell was used. In any of these choices, the selected area of shell ultimately placed certain restrictions on the final shape and size of the adze. For those adzes manufactured from the margin of the *Tridacna* valve, for example, a portion of the original valve or dorsal surface, including the whorl pattern, generally remains visible. This area is thinner than the rest of the valve, and as such presents a limit to the number of variations in the shape of the poll and bit, as well as treatment of the shell surface (the whorl pattern, for example, cannot be fully erased

without structurally compromising the tensile strength of the adze). Adzes fashioned from the dorsal/valve region of *Tridacna* are also limited in their range of variability and are in general long, narrow and relatively thick implements; while those from the hinge region are as unrestricted in shape and size as adzes manufactured from stone (Rosendahl 1987, Moir 1986-87). For hinge region adzes, much of the variability occurs not only in the poll and bit or cutting edge shape, but also in the cross-section.

The actual process of manufacture has been inferred from production debitage—flaking debris, blanks, and preforms (Kirch and Yen 1982, Rosendahl 1987, Osborne 1979, Beardsley 1994, 1997b)—and is best described as a series of continuous stages punctuated by landmarks or points of reference useful in visualizing the progress of the fashioning process. The whole process begins by roughing out a subrectangular blank using a hammer (either stone or shell), followed by continued flaking which gradually shifts from an initial hard hammer percussive force to more controlled techniques using soft hammer and indirect percussion, pressure flaking, pecking and grinding until the final finished adze form emerges. In terms of manufacturing stages, the blank, the first stage, is simply a roughed-out piece of stock material. It is portable and can easily be moved from the raw material source to a workshop setting (Figure 22).

The next stage in the manufacturing process, the preform, presents a more refined adze-shaped implement than the blank; in other words, the article is starting to take form and actually looks like an adze, or an approximation of an adze albeit unfinished (Figure 22). Preforms are, in essence, adzes in outline form. With stone, the difference between blanks and preforms lies in the techniques used to fashion each—blanks are formed primarily by percussion whereas preforms are shaped by a variety of methods including percussion, pressure flaking, pecking, and grinding. The difference between shell blanks and preforms is essentially the same; for shell, however, another reduction technique should be added to the reduction repertoire—cutting or sawing—the method used to split many gastropods (e.g., *Terebra* or *Mitra*) selected for adze production. From preforms collected on Kwajalein (Beardsley 1994), it appears that the preform outline was generally rectangular for dorsal/valve and margin region adzes and rectangular to trapezoidal for hinge region adzes, and that the poll and bit or cutting edge was among the last features fashioned on these implements. The final stage in the manufacturing process is the finished adze.

Attributes. The attributes recorded for each of the Safonfok adzes are summarized in Tables 2, 3, and 4. In general, the attributes are divided into four broad categories—provenience, metrical attributes, indices, and morphology. Provenience and the metrical data are self-

Figure 22. Adze perform (l) and blank (r), dorsal and ventral views.

explanatory and need no explanation. The third category, indices, is derived from the metrical data and is used primarily for comparative purposes on whole adze specimens only. Kirch and Yen (1982: 213, Figure 84) produced a visual interpretation of each index scale. According to their diagram, the thickness to width (T/W) index is anchored to a baseline value of 0.5 which refers to adzes with an elliptical transverse cross-section, whereas values less than 0.5 tend toward rectangular sections and those greater than 0.5 tend toward squared sections. The thickness to length (T/L) index refers to the section along the main axis of the implement, with a value of 0.5 referring to a shape that is twice as long as it is thick; anything less than 0.5 refers to a longer narrower shape, while values greater than 0.5 tend toward shorter, broader implements. The width to length (W/L) index is similar to the T/L index and refers to outline shapes ranging from narrow, long implements (less than 0.5) to short, wide implements (greater than 0.5). Finally, the taper index, which refers to the angle of the laterals from bit to poll, ranges from rectangular (less than 0.5) to trapezoidal (0.5) to triangular (greater than 0.5).

Morphology, the fourth category of attributes, tends to be more descriptive, referring principally to the condition of the adze. One of these features, Degree of Grinding, refers to one of five descriptions adapted from Butler (1988): no grinding; minimal grinding which is defined as lightly ground; medium grinding which means that the sides and high dorsal ridges (particularly on *Tridacna* specimens) are smoothed; extensive grinding means that nearly all surface features have been removed; and total grinding means that all natural surface features have been removed. The attribute of Edges Flaked is applicable only to blanks and preforms, and refers to the number of edges from which trimming flakes have been removed; it is one of the principal vehicles used in describing the manufacturing process. The last attribute, Type, refers to one of several adze types developed by Kirch and Yen (1982) and amended by Beardsley (1994). It is the primary means of making one collection comparable to others in the western Pacific; unfortunately, it is only useful with finished adzes—whole adzes, poll fragments of *Tridacna* hinge region adzes, and non-*Tridacna* adzes made from *Cassis, Conus, Terebra,* and *Mitra* shell.

Following Kirch and Yen (1982: 222, Figure 88), Type 1 adzes are micro-adzes less than 40 mm in length; Types 2 to 8 are *Tridacna* adzes with Types 2 to 5 referring to poll shape on dorsal/valve and margin region adzes and Types 6 to 8 directed to the cross-sections of hinge region adzes. A Type 2 adze displays minimal grinding; Type 3 adzes have blunt or rounded polls; Type 4 adzes have pointed polls; and Type 5 adzes have beveled polls. For the hinge region adzes, Type 6 refers to adzes with plano-convex cross-sections; Type 7 adzes have elliptical-oval cross-sections; and Type 8 adzes have quadrangular cross-sections. Types 9 and 10 are *Cassis* adzes manufactured in the former instance from the lip of the *Cassis* shell, and in the latter from the shell whorl. *Conus* shell adzes are Kirch and Yen's last type, Type 11. Amendments to this typology were developed to accommodate other shell species used in the manufacture of adzes, particularly in Micronesia. To accommodate these additional species, Types 12 (*Terebra*) and 13 (*Mitra*) have been added to the typology (Beardsley 1994).

Table 2. Adze Attributes

| CATEGORY | ATTRIBUTES |
|---|---|
| | |
| Provenience | Catalogue Number, Catalogue Number, Excavation Area, Trench/Grid Unit, Feature, Layer, Depth (cm bs) |
| Metrical Attributes | Length (mm), Width/Diameter (mm) across bevel-midsection-poll, Thickness (mm), Bevel Angle (deg), Weight (g) |
| Indices (whole specimens only) | Thickness/Width (T/W), Thickness/Length (T/L), Width/Length (W/L), Taper [(bev width − poll width)/length] |
| Morphology | Material (shell type), Status (whole/frag), Morphology (part of shell body used in manufacturing process), Grinding (degree of grinding), Transverse Section (e.g., plano-convex), Bevel Edge (straight, curved), Poll Morphology (e.g., blunt or rounded), Edges Flaked (for blanks and performs only), Type (for finished adzes only) |

Safonfok Adzes. The adzes recovered from Safonfok include six complete adzes (four *Terebra*, two *Tridacna*), one fragmentary adze (*Tridacna* bevel fragment), two preforms (both *Tridacna*) and two blanks (*Tridacna* and *Hippopus*) (Figure 23). A scattering of *Tridacna* flakes throughout the vertical and horizontal dimensions of the buried midden deposit, as well as a concentration of flaking debris in the Unit 5 area of the site, attest to an on-site production system for *Tridacna* adzes and by extension the production of adzes from other shell types. The Safonfok artifact assemblage can also add an even earlier step in the whole manufacturing process—the initial reduction of *Tridacna* valves to produce workable core fragments. The recovery of a basalt sledge hammer located in direct association with several *Tridacna* valves, many of which displayed the tell-tale signs of reduction in the form of negative flaking scars, has expanded the various stages in this production process.

The two blanks are roughly quadrangular in form: one is a long narrow flake from the valve section of *Tridacna*, with all evidence of surface features removed from both the ventral and dorsal faces; the second is an entire *Hippopus* valve with edges neatly chipped to give the implement an approximate adze-like shape. Both preforms are fashioned from a *Tridacna* valve, with one virtually whole and displaying an ovoid form. Its edges are neatly chipped to form a single continuous perimeter; there are no abrupt changes in lateral orientation, no corners, no bevel, no poll, and no grinding on any surface. The second preform is fragmentary, but contains a finely ground edge, with the highest points on the dorsal surface ground flat and a quadrangular cross-section.

Of the three finished *Tridacna* adzes, two are from the valve region and one is from the hinge. One of the valve region adzes is fragmentary, the bevel end, with a quadrangular cross-section, extensive grinding to shape both laterals and plane the dorsal and ventral surfaces, and a straight bevel edge. As this specimen is lacking a poll, no Type could be assigned. The second valve region adze is assigned to Type 3, owing to its blunted poll, straight (but damaged) bevel edge, and quadrangular cross-section.

The hinge region *Tridacna* adze is a finely fashioned specimen, with no surface features present on any face. It displays a relatively rounded poll, curved bevel edge, plano-convex cross-section, and has been totally ground. This adze is categorized as Type 6.

*Terebra* adzes make up the remaining completed inventory of adzes at Safonfok. All are assigned to Type 12, as they have been fashioned from the entire shell. All *Terebra* adzes have plano-convex cross-sections, curved bevel edges and just enough grinding to fashion the ventral face of the implement. No manipulation of the poll end of these implements is apparent, leaving untouched the natural pointed end of the shell itself.

Finally, a basalt sledge-hammer identified and recovered from the site is included here, as it represents the very initial stages of adze manufacture—reducing large, thick valves of *Tridacna* into smaller, more manageable pieces. The sledge-hammer is subrectangular in shape, with a battered rounded working end that still retains traces of shell embedded in the open pores, crevices and crannies common to the stone surface (Figure 24). At roughly the mid-line of the implement, a channel has been pecked around the entire circumference. This channel, it is surmised, likely provided a stable point to affix a cord around the implement and aid in its attachment to a tripod-sort of mechanism. Such an arrangement would allow gravity to contribute to the force of the sledge, allowing it to hang from its mount in order to more efficiently swing or direct its blows onto the item to be reduced. Several fractured and flaked *Tridacna* valves were located in the immediate vicinity of the sledge, further reinforcing this hypothetical functional reconstruction.

Comparisons. Comparisons of adze types across the western Pacific are spotty at best, and rely heavily on previously reported and analyzed specimens. Hinge

Figure 23. Shell adzes from Safonfok: a.,b. *Tridacna* adzes, dorsal and ventral views; c.,d. *Terebra* adzes, dorsal and ventral views.

region adzes, for example, are widely represented and are generally considered early types associated with Lapita-like assemblages, according to Kirch and Yen (1982); although ethnographic data has suggested hinge region adzes have continued to be used well into the historic era. Dorsal/valve region adzes also have a wide distribution across the western Pacific and occur in both early and late contexts (Kirch and Yen 1982). For Safonfok, that simply translates into a general prehistoric/traditional era occurrence of *Tridacna* adzes. As they appear in both early and late contexts, their presence at the site offers no real chronological value or context.

For non-*Tridacna* adzes, *Cassis* whorl adzes have been reported from eastern Micronesia, from Nukuoro and the Marshall group, while the *Cassis* lip adzes have been reported from western Micronesia (Kirch and Yen 1982); unfortunately, no chronological tags have been affixed to either type. *Terebra* adzes were not included in Kirch and Yen's typology, yet these adzes occur at Safonfok and other sites in Kosrae (Athens 1995); in both Palau and Kosrae, they appear to be concurrent with *Cassis* shell adzes (Athens 1995, Beardsley 1994, 1996, 1997a). According to Osborne (1966, 1979), *Terebra* shell adzes (his Type 1) are found on the southern limestone islands and low islands of Palau, while *Tridacna* adzes are widely distributed throughout Palau and other high islands. One could infer from this that *Terebra* and possibly *Cassis* adzes are predominately low island implements (though with no chronometric associations), while *Tridacna* adzes tend to dominate the assemblages throughout all islands, both high and low.

As chronological markers, particularly for Kosrae, there are still too few records of adzes in stratified, well-dated contexts. Most adzes have been recovered from surface

Table 3. Summary of Metrical Attributes for Safonfok Adzes

| CatNr | Provenience | Metrical Attributes (mm) | | | | | | | Indices | | | |
|-------|-------------|------|------|------|-------|------|-------|--------|------|------|------|-------|
| | | Len | BevW | MidW | PollW | Th | BvAng | Wgt(g) | T/W | T/L | W/L | Taper |
| 302-1 | Surface | 59.7 | 20.9 | 16.6 | 2.6 | 13.4 | 51 | 11.9 | 0.8 | 0.2 | 0.3 | 0.3 |
| 591-2 | Surface | 74.8 | 32.3 | 27.4 | 3.8 | 20.7 | 44 | 18.9 | 0.8 | 0.3 | 0.4 | 0.4 |
| 222 | Surface | 70.8 | 28.3 | 26.2 | 4.1 | 18.5 | 50 | 28.5 | 0.7 | 0.3 | 0.4 | 0.3 |
| 221 | Surface | 69 | 34.1 | 27.3 | 8 | 21.9 | 48 | 35.7 | 0.8 | 0.3 | 0.4 | 0.4 |
| 563 | Surface | 57.7 | 51.8 | 41/4 | 26 | 10.9 | 47 | 44.8 | -- | -- | -- | -- |
| 553 | Surface | 64.1 | 36.3 | 35.9 | 24.3 | 12.5 | -- | 58.6 | -- | -- | -- | -- |
| 571 | Surface | 113.2 | 57.6 | 56.3 | 39.6 | 21 | 53 | 202.8 | 0.4 | 0.2 | 0.5 | 0.2 |
| 561 | Surface | 115.3 | 49.6 | 59.6 | 49.6 | 13.7 | -- | 159.8 | 0.2 | 0.1 | 0.5 | 0.2 |
| 218-1 | U14L2 | 94.9 | -- | 41.6 | -- | 14.3 | -- | 68.2 | -- | -- | -- | -- |
| 218-2 | U14L2 | 45.1 | 68.6 | 57.5 | 39.2 | 11.7 | -- | 51.9 | -- | -- | -- | -- |
| 555-3 | Surface | 65.4 | -- | 109.1 | -- | 8.2 | -- | 75.1 | -- | -- | -- | -- |

Table 4. Summary of Morphological Attributes for Safonfok Adzes.

| CatNr | Material | Status | Morph | Grind | TransSect. | Bevel Edge | PollMorph | EdgeFlake | Type |
|-------|----------|--------|-------|-------|------------|------------|-----------|-----------|------|
| 302-1 | *Terebra* | Whole | Whorl | Minimal | Plano-convex | Curved | Pointed | None | 12 |
| 591-2 | *Terebra* | Whole | Whorl | Minimal | Plano-convex | Curved | Pointed | None | 12 |
| 222 | *Terebra* | Whole | Whorl | Minimal | Plano-convex | Curved | Pointed | None | 12 |
| 221 | *Terebra* | Whole | Whorl | Minimal | Plano-convex | Curved | Pointed | None | 12 |
| 563 | *Tridacna* | Bevel | Valve | Extensive | Quadrangular | Straight | Unknown | None | -- |
| 553 | *Tridacna* | Whole | Valve | Medium | Quadrangular | Straight | Blunt | None | 3 |
| 571 | *Tridacna* | Whole | Hinge | Total | Plano-convex | Curved | Rounded | None | 6 |
| 561 | *Tridacna* | Preform | Valve | None | -- | -- | -- | All | -- |
| 218-1 | *Tridacna* | Blank | Valve | None | -- | -- | -- | 5 | -- |
| 218-2 | *Tridacna* | Preform | Valve | Minimal | -- | -- | -- | 2 | -- |
| 555-3 | *Hippopus* | Blank | Valve | None | -- | -- | -- | 3 | -- |

contexts (Athens 1995), which bring to question their associations with traditional and prehistoric deposits. At Safonfok, a *Tridacna* blank and preform fragment (cat. nrs. 218-1, 218-2) were recovered from a level in the buried midden deposit dated between about A.D. 1400 and 1600; all other specimens were recovered from surface contexts.

**Ornaments, Shell Beads and their Manufacture**

A small number of beads—both finished and unfinished—were recovered from surface contexts and the excavations across Safonfok, along with debris from the manufacturing process and what appears to be at least one shell drill that made use of the natural attributes of a *Lambis*. This is in keeping with previous excavations on

Figure 24. Tools for adze production: a. basalt sledge and battered *Tridacna* valves (cores) *in situ*; b. *Tridacna* core showing battering scars; c. basalt sledge hammer.

Kosrae, where a variety of shell ornaments including beads, pendants, and possible bracelets, bangles and armbands have been recovered (Athens 1995, Cordy 1993, Sarfert 1919, Weisler 2001). Shells such as *Conus literatus*, *Spondylus*, *Trochus niloticus*, *Tectus pyramis*, and *Tridacna maxima* have often served as the raw materials for these ornaments; unfortunately, in most instances, shell type cannot be identified because the methods of manufacture—mainly grinding to finish and polish—tend to erase any tooling and fashioning marks.

Ornaments on Kosrae, as in other parts of the Pacific (Beardsley 1994, Butler 1988, Kirch and Yen 1982, Rosendahl 1987), have often been treated as monetary valuables, grave goods and heirloom specimens. Sarfert (1919), for example, described the historical use of disc beads made from *Tridacna* and *Spondylus*, along with beads made from coconut, as valuables worn mostly by men. His observation was further reinforced when Hambruch (Sarfert 1919) recovered several necklace fragments, or beads, from Leluh tombs. Most of these beads were manufactured from red *Spondylus*, although some appeared to be produced from pearl shell. Cordy (1993) too described the recovery of a number of shell beads during his excavations at Leluh, and commented that most of the beads and other ornaments (e.g., shell bracelets) were recovered from tombs, although a

scattered isolated few were found outside the tombs. The beads and bangles recovered by Athens (1995) came from excavations and surface surveys throughout the Leluh complex, and from sites in Tafunsak and Utwe.

Nearly all the beads from previous excavations were described as round or disc-shaped. The Safonfok beads, however, diverge from this norm (if round, disc-shaped beads can be considered the norm). Though few in number, the finished beads here display a range of shapes, including a bevel-edged diamond shape, a teardrop shape and the ubiquitous rounded disc-shape (Figure 25). All of these beads have a single bi-conical hole drilled through their centers. Their surfaces are ground and polished in the finishing stages. Identification of shell types is tentative at best, although the diamond and teardrop shaped beads appear to be manufactured from either *Trochus* or *Tectus*, while the rounded disc-shaped bead appears to be *Tridacna*.

Fragments of cut shell—mainly *Trochus* and *Tectus*—were recovered throughout Safonfok, usually concentrated in workshop/midden areas (both surface and subsurface), where the beads and other artifacts were also recovered. At least one of these cut shell fragments was described as a bead preform. The edges of the roughed-out polygonal form were cut along some sections and

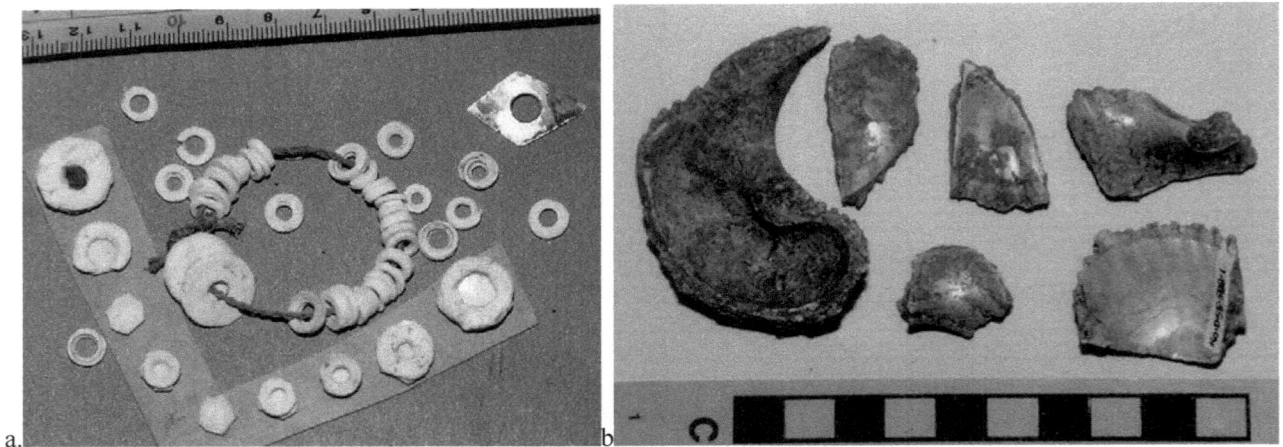

Figure 25. Shell beads: a. beads on display in the Kosrae Museum, including diamond-shaped bead recovered from Safonfok; b. shell fragments from bead production process; below, more beads and a bead perform from Safonfok.

chipped along other segments. Much of the dorsal surface detail was obscured by grinding, which created a relatively flat face; whereas, no finishing or grinding work was evident on the ventral face. A hole was drilled through the center of the rough-out, with drilling initiated from the dorsal side. Here the hole formed a conical entrance into and through the shell. On the ventral face, where the drill bit emerged, the edges of the hole appeared ragged as the uneven ends of the shell laminae were exposed.

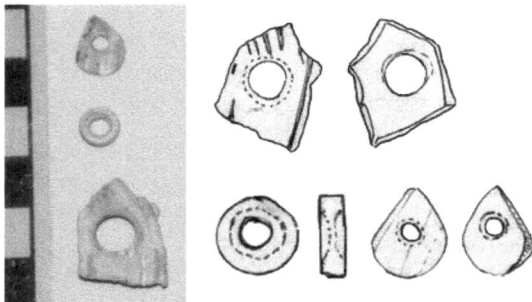

Manufacture. From this one preform alone, the process of bead manufacture can be inferred. It began with the preparation of a somewhat flat, roughed-out tab or polygonal shape that would eventually be transformed into a more refined shape. The outer surface would be ground flat, removing much, though not all surface features, at which point a hole would be drilled through the approximate center from the outer surface. Finishing work on the bead would likely involve smoothing the ventral edge of the hole to remove any jagged edges; this would in turn create a bevel and in essence produce what would appear to be a bi-conical hole. The final shaping of the bead itself would then follow, with the edges of the roughed-out tab ground as necessary.

What, however, would be used to produce the hole in the center of the bead? The production of a conical, beveled hole would require a spiral motioned drill. Would the tip of a coral fishhook-like implement be an appropriate tool? Coral is often used as an abrader in shaping and finishing work, but to cut a hole through a small flat fragment of shell? A more appropriate and denser material may be another shell. A number of *Lambis* shells, mostly bodies without the extensive network of arms that form the lip of this gastropod, were recovered in direct association with the cut shell fragments (Figure 26a). In fact, it was a predictable association; whenever cut *Trochus* or *Tectus* was observed, a *Lambis* shell would usually be close by, if not in direct association with the mix of shell fragments. One of the *Lambis* in particular was identified as a drill. The lip had been removed, chipped off, with only one point remaining at its distal end. This point displayed characteristic spiral-like marks that suggested its use as a drill.

To test this interpretation, one of our crew members picked up another *Lambis* from the site, along with the valve of a small clam and drilled a hole through the valve, entering from its dorsal surface (Figure 26b). It was an easy process, requiring little expenditure of energy. The result was a beveled hole, roughly the same diameter as holes in at least two of the beads (3 mm; the other bead and preform have slightly larger holes than this). The exit edge of the hole, on the ventral side of the valve, was jagged, just as the hole on the bead preform discussed above.

**Abraders and Abraded Coral**

Coral abraders, along with a small collection of abraded coral fragments, were observed and collected throughout the project area—from the surface and subsurface. Virtually all specimens in this category are lobed, globular coral fragments, which display various shapes

54

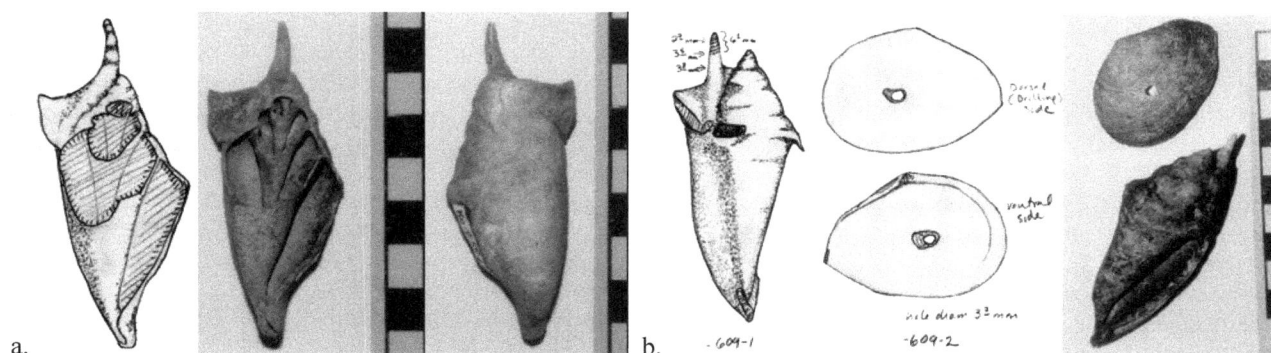

Figure 26. *Lambis* drills: a. archaeological specimen recovered from Safonfok; b. drilling experiment

owing to their abraded surfaces (Figure 27). The abraders fall into two basic categories, according to the visible characteristics of their worked facets: 1) narrow, angular forms such as files, distinguished by adjacent ground facets that form sharp beveled edges at the intersection, and 2) cobble forms distinguished by the retention of their lobed, cobble-like form but with flat grinding facets present (Rosendahl [1987] also recognized these two basic shapes in coral abraders recovered throughout the Marshall Islands). Abraded coral, on the other hand, are simply fragments of coral fortuitously used in grinding or abrading activity. They display no formal shape, nor systematically fashioned grinding facets; instead, they display random striations and lanes of grinding.

The cobble abraders are generally ovate in shape, with rounded surfaces. All of these abraders were shaped by grinding, as their surfaces were uniformly smooth with little or no natural features remaining. Their use as formal tools appears to be confined to one of the slightly rounded faces. One cobble abrader (nr. 58) exhibited unique features, which led us to speculate about its use in woodworking activities such as finishing canoes. It retained a single ground leveled face, much like a cross-section through its globular form, along with the impressions of the hand and fingers that gripped the tool. The finger impressions consisted predominately of discrete zones of slightly depressed, slightly ovate, crushed coral with a slight patina. Holding the implement further reinforces the grip; no matter which way the tool is turned in your hand, it inevitably winds up in the same position time and time again—always the right hand, always the same grip. Its working face is broad and flat, suggesting further that is was used on a broad flat surface, which could potentially be an indirect reference to activities such as canoe working or refining structural walls, beams or other structural features.

Angular abraders take on the shape and look of knife-like implements, where two adjoining faces meet in a narrow, acute angle. Their use as knives is unlikely, as any concentrated use along the edge would quickly diminish

its effectiveness owing to the soft grainy quality of the coral itself. However, abrading use on the facets, either alone or together, is highly likely and suggested by the striations appearing on these faces.

The actual articles, tools, or materials intended as the recipients of abrading activities remain the subject of pure speculation, mostly. Shell beads, for example, display narrow striations across their surfaces suggesting abrasion as a finishing technique with coral as the principal material in their final shaping. Coral fishhooks and shell adzes, too, exhibit abrasion scars from their finishing process; again, coral is implicated as the material used for the abrading. Unfortunately, other materials, such as wood, have not survived the test of time and as such dampen any suppositions regarding further use of coral abraders. Coral abraders and abraded coral appear in archaeological inventories across Micronesia, in the Marshall Islands (Beardsley 1994, Rosendahl 1987; Riley 1987, Streck 1990, Craib 1989), Palau and the Marianas (Athens 1986, Beardsley 1996, 1997a, Sarfert 1919, Shun and Athens 1990). In fact, its appearance in these assemblages indicates it was a common material used in the production process.

### Worked Shell, Ground Pumice and Cut Charcoal

This catch-all category includes a variety of artifacts that do not seem to fit into any other groups—used shell flakes, shell food scrapers, pumice with a ground 'abrasion' facet, and fragments of cut and drilled charcoal (Figure 28). Shell flakes, particularly produced during the reduction of *Tridacna*, provide useful, expedient tools for cutting, scraping, sawing, and shaving. Such activities leave in their wake a series of striations along with micro-fractures produced along the working edge of the flake tool. The flakes themselves do not require additional modification other than a cursory refinement (as needed) of a working edge; generally, the edges produced through the process of reduction and separation are usually sufficient.

Shell food scrapers also need little refinement in their production. A simple rounded to ovoid hole near the hinge of a bivalve shell provides the necessary working edge for these implements. Shell graters or scrapers are a common tool across the Pacific, appearing in both archaeological and ethnographic assemblages (Beardsley 1994, Kirch and Yen 1982, Osborne 1966, 1979, Rosendahl 1987, Sarfert 1919, Shun and Athens 1990, Spoehr 1957). They are used principally to remove the skin from roots and tubers—an action that tends to increase the ovoid shape of the orifice. The Safonfok specimens, particularly those with elongated, ovate openings, exhibit scars from scraping and grating. The scars appear at opposite ends of the ovate openings, and appear ground and slightly beveled with some striations as well as an occasional flake removed from these working edges. Without exception, the shell scrapers appear to be used in a side to side movement that runs at a right angle to the axis of this shellfish (one where the hinge provides the orienting factor).

Figure 27. Coral abraders of various shapes. Lower abrader (ventral and dorsal views) retains grip impressions of hand that held and used the implement.

Pumice may or may not have been available on Kosrae during the traditional era; however, reliance on coral for abrading as opposed to pumice suggests its availability as a raw material was limited. Its appearance on the island and in the Safonfok artifact assemblage is likely the result of an unpredictable series of events that relied on random wave patterns and various currents to carry the

material from one place to the next across the open waters of the Pacific. A fragment of water-rolled pumice was recovered in the Safonfok assemblage, from the midden deposit that characterizes the principal period of occupation. The pumice retains an abraded facet (the working face) and three principal concavities that seem to have accommodated the grip of a left-handed person. There are no residuals of use-wear visible on the tool, as pumice is, by its very nature, a lot like coral with a highly porous and very rough surface.

Within the charcoal recovered from the site midden, several fragments displayed the residues of workmanship that best characterizes an artifact production industry. Most of the fragments are coconut, though at least a couple are of an unidentified wood and one is a nutshell. All fragments display either drilling, cutting, notching, or remnants of puncture-like holes. Many of the cuts are sinuous, with some fragments reminiscent of the debris from fishhook manufacture. No actual fishhooks were recovered; however, as coconut is one of several materials from which fishhooks were made (Anell 1955, Beasley 1928, Emory, Bonk and Sinoto 1959), we cannot rule out the possibility that at least some of these charcoalized remains are somehow related to fishhook manufacture.

**Flaked Stone and Shell**

By sheer numbers alone, flaked stone and shell are one of the more common artifacts in the Safonfok assemblage, after the coral debitage from the manufacture of fishhooks. Both flaked stone and shell were recovered during excavations and surface surveys, always in association with the midden matrix that defined site occupation. Much of the recovered flaked stone consisted of heat shattered cobbles suspended throughout the midden matrix, the apparent result of *um* rake-outs; however, at least two deliberately flaked formal stone implements were also recovered. The amount of flaked shell scattered throughout the site simply reinforced the role of shell as a raw material in the manufacturing process—to produce beads, adzes, drills, and other implements, ornaments and articles. All the flaked shell under this category would be classified as debitage (outside of those flaked specimens identified as utilized/expedient tools or as part of the early stages of adze manufacture). None of these flakes exhibit any directed modification and are best described as by-products of the manufacturing/reduction process.

One of the flaked stone implements is an adze-like chopper fashioned from a very fine-grained basalt (Figure 29). It was recovered from the surface within one of the attached but exterior rooms of Safonfok, in direct association with a deep-troughed grinding stone or mortar (also of basalt—a coarse grained basalt). The working edge of the chopper was formed by flaking, rather than grinding. Damage visible along this edge—blunted with random flaking—betrays a use involved in

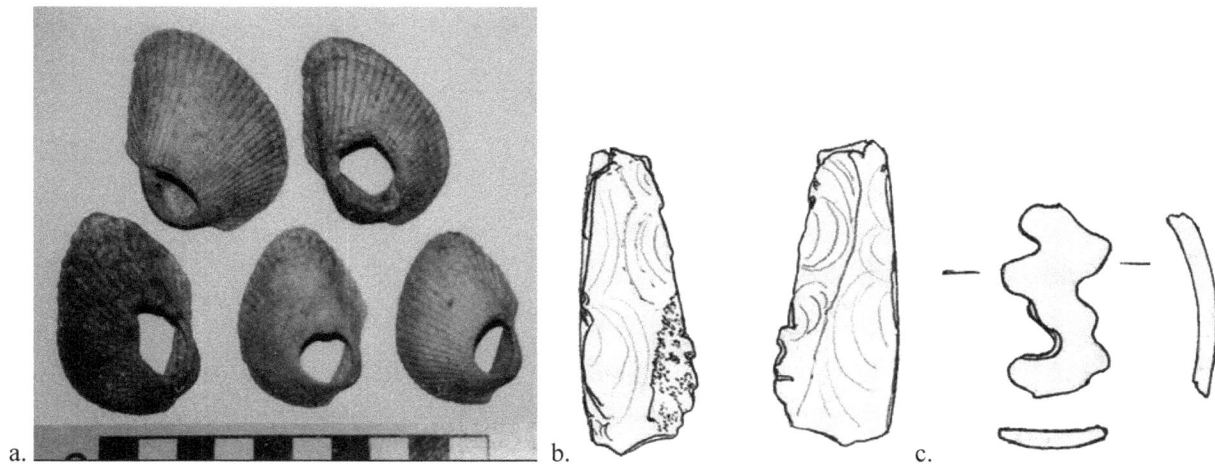

Figure 28. Worked shell and coconut: a. food scrapers; b. utilized shell flake with one lateral edge ground flat, the other used in a knife-like slicing fashion (43.9 x 17x 3.1 mm); c. carbonized cut coconut shell.

processing, cutting, dicing, even scraping plants and plant parts. Hafting scars are visible on the edges and protrusions of the tool, with hafting apparently covering the poll half of the implement  Our interpretation of this tool, its association with a grinding stone, as well as the outer room in which it was found, was that all three were associated with the medicine specialist's domain. This interpretation was based solely on local knowledge, as one of the crew members was from a family that 'owns' local medicine. He recognized these implements almost immediately, explaining how his grandmother used similar tools when she made her medicine. As if to complement this interpretation and further reinforce the medicinal association, medicinal plants were growing in large numbers throughout the site with the greatest density concentrated in and around the medicine specialist's enclosure. Further observations made on a more casual basis bolstered our interpretation—within this part of the island, Safonfok was the only historical site where such plants occurred.

The second formal flaked stone tool was a triangular backed knife, also of fine grained basalt (Figure 30). It was, unfortunately, represented by two fragments rather than a complete specimen. Yet, the two fragments were sufficient to illustrate their fabrication and even use. The knife was fashioned along natural laminae fractures in the basalt. Two of the three faces converged to form an acute angle that served as the working edge of the implement, with one of the two faces bearing the residues of having been minimally ground. The third face forms the back of the knife; the edge that would serve as the handle and the place from which pressure could be exerted to more efficiently take advantage of the working edge. Its shape is reminiscent of breadfruit cleavers seen on the island today.

Of all the flaked shell recovered from the site, the most revealing in terms of activities conducted at Safonfok were a series of *Tridacna* flakes confined to the Unit 5 area—inferred as a workshop for the reduction of *Tridacna* cores. In the field, this area was referred to as the 'adze workshop' because it had very little midden, yet supported a dense concentration of *Tridacna* flakes. No other part of the site contained such a concentration of *Tridacna* debris.

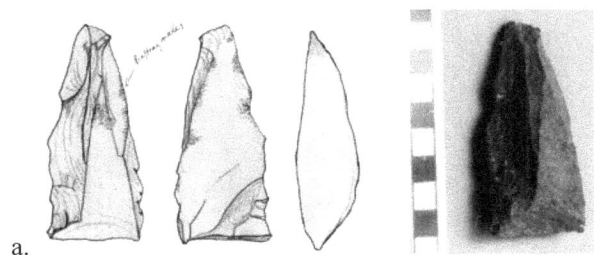

Figure 29. Basalt medicine chopper and *in situ* mortar with which it was associated.

The flaked shell generally illustrates the importance of production discard. It is from such artifacts, none of which display any directed manipulation or shaping, that the technology of a culture becomes evident. At Safonfok, the flaked shell debitage indicates an industry that made use of production techniques centered on cutting, grinding, drilling, and flaking; some of the tools used in this process have been discussed in previous sections. When placed next to any of the finished shell articles, the full extent of the shell working industry becomes evident, from the selection and initial reduction of shell (*Tridacna*, *Terebra*, *Lambis*, *Trochus*, *Tectus*, and so on) to the intermediate stages in which an ornament, tool, or other article gradually takes shape, to the finishing stages of grinding and polishing, and finally to the later stages of use and discard. The sequence is unmistakable, presenting a legible text on this tool making industry that can be 'read' by most anyone reviewing the overall artifact assemblage. What should also be evident in such a review is the overall lack of stone debitage, other than heat shattered rock associated with *um* rake-outs. Stone was not a raw material of choice; marine resources such as coral and shell were. In category after category, marine resources dominate; stone is virtually absent with the exception of a sledge hammer, a medicinal chopper, a basalt knife, and a scattering of heat-shattered *um* rocks.

Figure 30. Basalt knife with missing section.

## Other, including *Seka* Stones in the Rubble

One artifact, the fragment of a coral tile, was recovered from the surface of the site. Both faces of the tile appear to be planed to form smooth, flat surfaces. The nature of surface planing is not consistent with traditional industries, suggesting this fragment is of a later (more recent) era. Planing appears to have been completed with a mechanical apparatus that was geared toward creating a smooth, even surface and a tile of consistent thickness. There are no visible gouges or striations on the artifact, while polyp surfaces appear almost compressed rather than sheared as one might expect with traditional technologies.

The second artifact type in this category is the *seka* stone, a basalt slab with shallow grooves ground into one face. These stones are traditionally used to make *seka* (elsewhere in the Pacific referred to as *sakau* or *kava*), a slightly narcotic ceremonial drink made from the root of the *piper* plant. All the *seka* stones associated with Safonfok were mixed into the wall rubble, though it is uncertain if they were actually part of the building material or added at a later date. Not one *seka* stone was identified within the site compound, or in any of the exterior rooms. At least three *seka* stones were observed, although several other possible (though unconfirmed) *seka* stones were espied buried in the wall rubble.

## Specialized Analyses

And so it continues. A number of specialized samples were collected over the course of excavations with the intent of submitting them for various analyses. Both charcoal and faunal specimens—bone and shell—were the principle focus of collection efforts, as they could be used for radiocarbon dating as well as species identification. The intent was to use these samples as a means of placing Safonfok into a specific chronological period (radiocarbon dating), as well as to examine and even compare the adequacy of dates derived from different kinds of materials (an optimistic search for alternative dating materials). Other kinds of information that may (and hopefully will) be derived from the specialized samples include a description of subsistence practices, environmental conditions during the principal episode of site occupation, resource zone exploitation, and even material culture recruitment. Both the charcoal and faunal samples were collected from subsurface features such as earth ovens, or *um*, and extracted from various levels in the midden deposit.

Only the radiocarbon dates have been returned, as specialists in wood charcoal analysis and faunal analysis have yet to complete their investigations. The dating results, however, were both interesting and informative. Dating samples with both integrity and clear cultural associations were selected for processing. Together, they produced a fairly tight sequence of heavy occupation between cal A.D. 1400 and 1600, with a lighter occupation indicated prior to that and beginning at least cal A.D. 1200 and quite possibly earlier. In essence, the dating of Safonfok has added another segment to the growing chronology of a cultural presence on Kosrae and further corroborated an increasingly complex island occupation from at least cal A.D. 1200 (and, as noted, perhaps earlier).

### Radiocarbon Dating

The Safonfok radiocarbon dates have indicated an intensive occupation from about cal A.D. 1400 to 1600, with an even earlier though lighter occupation of the site area beginning at least cal A.D. 1200 (and more than likely earlier than that). All twenty radiocarbon samples submitted for dating were drawn from stratigraphic locations with both integrity and cultural associations.

Table 5. Radiocarbon Dates, Safonfok, Kosrae

| SampleNr. | LabNr. | Provenience | | Mat'l | $C^{14}$ type | Date BP | $\delta^{13}C$ | cal Date AD (2 σ range) |
|---|---|---|---|---|---|---|---|---|
| 29 | Wk-9475 | U2/3 *um* | I/II | charcoal | standard | 306 ± 58 | -26.2 ± 0.2 | 1440 –1670 AD 1780 –1800 AD |
| 48 | Wk-9476 | U4, L3 | II | shell | standard | 1254 ± 51 | 0.1 ± 0.2 | 1180 –1420 AD |
| 49 | Wk-9477 | U4. L4 | II | shell | standard | 959 ± 52 | 0.9 ± 0.2 | 1420 –1660 AD |
| 53 | Wk-9478 | U4, L3 | II | charcoal | standard | 451 ± 71 | -26.2 ± 0.0 | 1320 –1350 AD 1390 –1640 AD |
| 55 | Wk-9479 | U4, L4 | II | charcoal | AMS | 363 ± 53 | -28.6 ± 0.2 | 1440 –1640 AD |
| 59s | Wk-9480 | U4, L5 | II | shell | standard | 1288 ± 53 | 0.9 ± 0.2 | 1130 –1410 AD |
| 59 | Wk-9481 | U4, L5 | II | charcoal | AMS | 297 ± 57 | -25.1 ± 0.2 | 1450 –1680 AD 1770 –1800 AD |
| 67(1) | Wk-9482 | U6, L2 | II | charcoal | standard | 235 ± 47 | -26.3 ± 0.0 | 1490 –1600 AD 1610 –1700 AD 1720 –1820 AD 1910 –1960 AD |
| 67(2) | Wk-9483 | U6, L2 | II | charcoal | standard | 409 ± 52 | -26.8 ± 0.2 | 1420 –1640 AD |
| 69 | Wk-9484 | U6, L1 | I/II | charcoal | standard | 268 ± 66 | -27.2 ± 0.2 | 1400 –1950 AD |
| 94 | Wk-11829 | U12, L2 | II | charcoal | standard | 348 ± 46 | -25.5 ± 0.2 | 1480 –1650 AD |
| 180 | Wk-11830 | U12, L4 | II | charcoal | AMS | 300 ± 43 | -26.6 ± 0.2 | 1470 –1670 AD |
| 197 | Wk-11831 | U16, L2 | II | charcoal | standard | 359 ± 49 | -26.0 ± 0.2 | 1440 –1640 AD |
| 198 | Wk-11832 | U16, L5 | III/IV | charcoal | AMS | 450 ± 41 | -25.9 ± 0.2 | 1400 –1520 AD 1590 –1620 AD |
| 199 | Wk-11833 | U16, L7 | IV | charcoal | AMS | 365 ± 41 | -24.8 ± 0.2 | 1440 –1640 AD |
| 200 | Wk-11834 | U16, L6 | IV | charcoal | AMS | 430 ± 41 | -25.4 ± 0.2 | 1410 –1530 AD 1580 –1630 AD |
| 211 | Wk-11835 | U16, L4 | III | charcoal | standard | 639 ± 79 | -26.0 ± 0.2 | 1240 –1440 AD |
| 212 | Wk-11836 | U16, L3 | II | charcoal | standard | 443 ± 51 | -25.7 ± 0.2 | 1400 –1530 AD 1560 –1640 AD |
| 440 | Wk-11837 | U28, L2 | II | charcoal | standard | 404 ± 52 | -25.7 ± 0.2 | 1420 –1640 AD |
| 463 | Wk-11838 | U27, L1 | 1/II | charcoal | standard | 239 ± 48 | -26.7 ± 0.2 | 1490 –1700 AD 1720 –1820 AD 1910 –1960 AD |

Of these samples, three sets consisted of paired shell and charcoal samples (an attempt to draw a correlation between the two in a never-ending search for alternative dating materials) and six AMS samples (accelerator mass spectrometry, i.e., samples too small for standard radiocarbon measurements). Table 5 summarizes the relevant information for each dating sample, including its stratigraphic position. Layer II, the midden deposit and principal occupational stratum, was the focus of most dating activity, with dates intended to bracket initial deposition, abandonment, and the timing of its most intensive period of use. Charcoal samples were also derived from each layer of the deepest unit on the site, Unit 16, which not only passed through the principal midden deposit but which was also part of the excavation block that exposed the buried coral spread interpreted as an earlier man-made pavement. The intent here was to place this leveled pavement into some kind of chronometric context; stratigraphically it is distinctly older than the principal site occupation as it rests in a position below the midden deposit. How much older, however, remained to be addressed.

Overall, the charcoal consisted of a variety of woody fuels, with pandanus keys, coconut shell and other woody debris dominating the mix. Additional wood charcoal identifications are underway, with results pending. The shell submitted for radiocarbon comparisons consisted primarily of a small clam, a common midden component at Safonfok and one which has been described as a significant component in middens prior to A.D. 500 (Athens 1995). Its ubiquity in the midden at Safonfok suggests it was a dominant focus of the site's subsistence regimen, representing a good many meals throughout the occupation of the site. As a mealtime residue, it also retains the status of having been a quick kill, with the animal meeting its demise within a short time prior to the preparation of the meal.

Taken together, the radiocarbon dates for Safonfok present a fairly tightly clustered pattern that extends from the 15th through 17th centuries, with two of the charcoal dates (53/WK9478 and 211/WK11835) extending occupation into the 13th and 14th centuries (Figure 31). Two shell dates extend the dating sequence even deeper into the past, into the 12th century (48/WK9476 and 59s/WK9480), while dates drawn from the transition

FIGURE **31**. SAFONFOK RADIOCARBON DATES IN GRAPH FORM

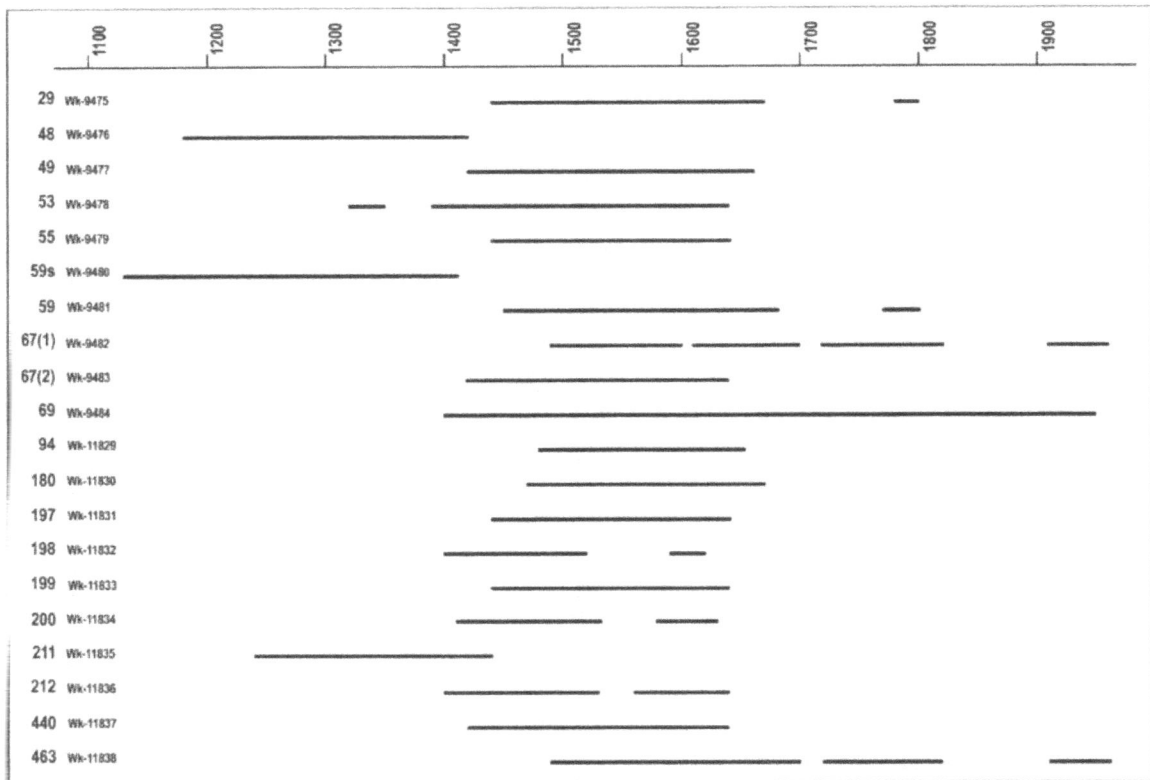

between Strata I and II bring site dates into the 20th century. What, however, does all this mean when placing Safonfok into a specific time frame? Dates from the 19th and 20th centuries likely reflect the post-traditional occupation of Safonfok, a time when the site was temporarily occupied by the shipwrecked Marshallese family. However, application of these late dates to the full, traditional occupation of Safonfok is inappropriate. Oral histories have intimated that Safonfok was abandoned well before known traditional histories, 'before the before' as local historians have reported. Even as a place name, Safonfok does not appear on the earliest Western maps of Kosrae; although other settlements and place names on this part of the southwest coastline do appear.

By expunging the later 19th and 20th century dates, the end of traditional occupation at Safonfok would be set sometime within the 17th century—a time frame supported by oral history and the artifact assemblage described above (i.e., no late, historic era artifacts were recovered from the site). But what of the dates of initial settlement? This particular issue is still unsettled. The charcoal dates suggest occupation by the 13th century, although the presence of a buried coral pavement below this date is tacit confirmation for a still earlier occupation in the site area. How much earlier remains problematic.

If the two early shell dates are applied to this matter, site occupation could be as early as the 12th century.

However, the buried coral pavement has yet to be placed into a more specific, bracketed time period, other than 'sometime before the 13th century.' Both early shell dates were derived from the midden deposit in the Unit 4 excavation area; not a location in the immediate vicinity of the coral pavement yet stratigraphically still above that pavement. Within the immediate area of the pavement, three radiocarbon samples were selected from the stratum immediate below it with the expectation that the dates would be useful in providing a dating cap for the pavement. They were, unfortunately of little help; all produced dates between the 15th and 17th centuries. At first glance, this was disconcerting, until a closer review of these three dates (198/WK11832, 199/WK11833, 200/WK11834)—all were AMS dates, which indicates the samples were quite small and as such very susceptible to downward vertical movement.

Like individual soil grains, charcoal and all other components suspended in a soil matrix are subject to up-and-down movement throughout the matrix; however, the actual rate and distance of movement depends on the size of the object relative to the size of all other objects nearby. In general, larger objects tend to move upward at a slower rate and a shorter distance, in much the same way that larger kernels of popcorn seem to float to the top of a bowl when it is shaken (the popcorn analogy). As the larger objects meet, gaps are formed between them; it is through these gaps that smaller objects (e.g., unpopped kernels, popcorn crumbs and fragments) fall and seem to move downward, accumulating at the bottom of the bowl. By extension, AMS charcoal samples ought to behave like those unpopped kernels et al., moving from the midden deposit above the pavement downward through and past (below) the coral cobble and pebble spread of the pavement itself. This makes their utility for dating the actual construction of the pavement suspect, leaving the timing of initial occupation in the site area unconfirmed.

Shell and Radiocarbon Dating. One of the goals of radiocarbon dating for Safonfok was to examine the correlation between paired shell and charcoal samples, each selected in close proximity to the other. Of the three pairs, only one produced anything like a close correspondence that fell within the principal period of occupation (49/WK9477 and 55/WK9479). The other two paired samples were consistent in their lack of correspondence; the shell dates were uniformly early, while the charcoal dates fell well within the dating range of the principal period of occupation. This unexpected result begs the question on the usefulness of shell as a dating medium. Why were two of the three shell samples so much earlier? Could they have been the subject of transport by crabs? Could their presence be the result of natural vertical movement? If the latter, then one would expect all shell in this general stratum to produce earlier dates than their charcoal pair. This leaves 'transport by crabs' as another possibility. As the excavation units have long been filled in, direct inspection of intrusive crab burrows throughout the unit is not an option, which leaves only field notes, photographs, stratigraphic profiles, the recovered sample itself, and memory by which to make this determination.

Virtually all the excavation blocks across Safonfok retained remnants of crab burrows; they seemed to be a fairly common occurrence throughout the life of the site occupation. The burrows, however, were not all active; many were abandoned, filled in and capped long ago by the succeeding stratum. Burrows throughout the midden, the main occupation stratum, were packed with mixed midden and little else—generally, the difference was small between the crab burrow midden and the midden of the surrounding matrix; the only real difference being a slightly different coloring and the presence of many more fine grained sediments in the burrows. Such burrows and their makers would provide a more expedient means of transporting or rather displacing midden, especially larger components like shell, throughout the entire deposit. So, could the dated shell samples be the result of crab transport? Indeed they could, although it will continue to remain speculation and hypothesis for now.

The uneven results of the shell-charcoal pairs does not bode well for shell as an alternative, in-lieu-of dating material for coastal sites such as Safonfok. However, as a supplement to charcoal dates, shell offers some insights into the timing of occupation that are not available (at least so far) from charcoal dates. The caveat for use would be to insure contemporaneity with the cultural deposit, and that kill dates for the shell are relatively close in time to their final discard. Shell for tool manufacture, particularly Tridacna, would not likely qualify as a suitable alternative, as it is often used in fossil form, making timing between the death and final discard indeterminate. But shell dates related specifically to consumption and subsistence practices do offer an advantage of sorts to the developing chronology of a site: they can be considered a source of hypothesis development and they can serve as a prompt in generating more effort toward identifying the earlier occupation of the site.

# VI. INTERPRETATIONS AND CONCLUSIONS

The archaeological record at Safonfok is a complex composite of a history expressed in varying degrees of decay and dismantlement. Accumulated over time in unknown increments, this record ranges from initial settlement through an era of intensive use to abandonment and the sundry post-occupation activities and events that ultimately brought the site into the current era. Peeling back these layers of time, from present to past, in order to understand and explain the nature of this particular historical record and its contribution to the broader patterns of history is the stuff of archaeology. Some might think this is an exercise in futility; a pure reflection of the paradox of archaeology, which is a discipline that concentrates on an archaeological record (often in tatters) existing in the current era while at the same time focusing on reconstructing those conditions, events and activities of the past responsible for creating that record. Yet, humanizing, explaining and reassembling the past through inferences drawn from tangible remains is precisely the goal of archaeology. For now, the human mind and soul are more or less unreachable, but the use of analogy and experiment often provides a suitable substitute. And when accompanied by liberal doses of oral history (where available), some semblance of the past emerges; one that is engaging and frequently reveals a once active occupation expressed in the routines of life, politics and everyday survival. At Safonfok, all the key elements are present, from a fishing industry focused on lagoonward and off-shore waters to medicine making, canoe construction, adze manufacture, and the production of more luxurious items linked to status and adornment but quite necessary to satisfy those creature comforts that fall into a whim shared by every one—the will to be fine (Boas 1929). There are also inklings of visits by dignitaries and tradesmen, and the presence of a local support staff attached to the site either through allegiance or the obligations of an indentured servitude. Safonfok was in its time a central place; a major administrative power and a market force to be reckoned with during the formative era in Kosrae history.

The first cultural use of Safonfok occurred sometime before A.D. 1200. By this time, the shoreline had prograded sufficiently to create an active beach fronting the lagoon with a stable back-beach deposit in place. Right at this transitional point, where the active beach meets the back-beach, evidence of human tenancy is inferred from the presence of a leveled coral spread. The exact timing for the appearance of this pavement remains unresolved. When it was initially laid; whether it was a natural deposit, or cultural. If it was natural, then what events were responsible for its origin? Stratigraphically, the pavement rests below the midden that forms the principal site deposit. But, when the strata below the midden were reviewed across the site, this particular pavement was the only feature of its kind—nowhere else were leveled compacted planes of coral encountered. This pavement was, in other words, an anomalous isolated event.

Could this have been the result of highly selective tidal events? Possibly. No artifacts were recovered in direct association with the pavement. At the same time, however, descriptions of random, isolated tidal events are difficult to find, as are descriptions of tidal events responsible for the formation of leveled hard-packed coral deposits. Tidal surges can and do deposit mixed strata of lagoonal debris, including coral, across beach fronts and coastal plains. But these deposits often contain a large mix of sand, with coral fragments suspended randomly throughout the matrix; rarely do they ever result in a well-sorted, leveled and compacted deposit of coral only. If natural agencies do not provide a reasonable and parsimonious explanation for the presence of this pavement, that leaves the prospects of cultural agencies. The structure of the pavement itself holds the ultimate insights into natural versus cultural processes. As a well compacted feature with larger corals lining the leveled surface and smaller nearly pebble sized corals packed between the cobbles and below this surface, this pavement exhibits a composition common to man-made coral pavements across the Pacific. Such pavements elsewhere are inferred evidence of human occupation; here in Safonfok, that would imply occupation on this part of the coastline, in this part of the site area some time before A.D. 1200. Unfortunately, the presence of this pavement does not tell us how people used the site area. Although one can assume it was used by fisherman and others who focused on the collection of marine resources.

With time, a permanent self-contained community was established in the site area, beginning sometime around A.D. 1200. Buildings, structures of various sorts, and the foundations of structures were raised. An organized community was established, settlement became denser, differential status markers were more visible, a high status administrative center emerged, and life itself played out daily, annually and according to the cycles of the sea and other natural events such as the ripening of breadfruit. At the height of occupation (the period of its most intensive use), between A.D. 1400 and 1600, Safonfok consisted of a large walled compound, among the largest on the island. This was the peak of the formative era on Kosrae, when political and social complexity were increasing alongside an intense rivalry between regional centers, each of which strived for control over the resources of the island. Safonfok was one of these competing centers, controlling an unknown area while vying to expand its own resource base and increase its areal dominance.

Both the size of Safonfok and its artifact assemblage, replete with high status articles, suggest an elite regional or district administrative center. Within the compound there are several cooking and workshop areas, each littered with the debris produced by various domestic laborers and artisans who were called upon to create the ornamental and utilitarian goods necessary to sustain and reinforce the position and rank of the site's elite residents. These elite members of society are those who donned the shell beads fashioned at the site, and who might have brokered the production of several distinctive tool types (e.g., shell adzes) or canoes. Scattered house foundations appear in various states of preservation throughout the site, but their specific functions remain unknown; analogies drawn from historic references suggest they could have been used as sleeping houses, meeting houses or entertainment houses. Outside the compound, within 20 meters of the site, an occupation appears in the form of dense midden and artifact scatters. These were perhaps residential areas housing a population in-service to the elite residents of the compound.

Immediately outside and adjacent to the compound wall are a series of enclosures separated by stone walls. The 'rooms' could have served as temporary quarters for visiting dignitaries or tradesmen, for their rest and repose after a long canoe journey—a pattern that would be in character with general Pacific Island practices. The enclosures could have also served in a secondary capacity, as a form of quarantine, allowing site residents sufficient time to determine the motives of the visitors, whether they were peaceful and well-intentioned or adversarial. At least one of the enclosures appears to have housed the medicine specialist; a service probably controlled by the elite residents of the site. Medicine and medicinal knowledge is restricted in the Pacific, not every one has access to it. Even in Kosrae today, only one or two families have access to traditional medicinal knowledge. The medicine specialist's enclosure is set apart from the site by its arrangement of walls; it is not easily accessible by either residents of the site or off-site visitors, and is oriented in such a way that it provides a degree of privacy not apparent in any of the other enclosures. Another enclosure, adjacent to the canoe landing, appears to contain features suggestive of an off-loading zone, where commodities transported into or away from the site by water were temporarily housed.

The high status of Safonfok is reinforced still further by its architecture and the extent of its encompassing compound wall. The wall likely reached a height of 2 to 3 meters and was constructed with multiple courses of coral and basalt. Several openings were built into its length and at least two niches were placed in the easternmost, mangrove facing wall. Aesthetic design elements include: the placement of large coral rounds flanking the entrance of only one of the several openings (this would have been the formal, official entry into the compound, intended to impress visitors); a coral and basalt veneer lining each opening; a well-planned, manicured pavement forming the outer walkways on the western, northern and eastern sides of the compound wall; an interior, single course pavement that forms an apron at the base of the compound wall; the presence of slope retaining walls and a paved canoe landing at the front (eastern) side of the compound. This canoe ramp was the official landing for Safonfok; it extended from the compound to the edge of the mangrove channel. Another, less elaborate canoe ramp further upstream is also present; however, its use solely by local residents or craftsmen attached to the Safonfok compound is postulated (and would be in keeping with local traditions; in a sense, it would be tantamount to a backdoor into the site).

By all appearances, Safonfok was an active administrative center at the peak of the formative era. Its size, features and artifact content belie both wealth and standing among its contemporaries, and it appears to have attracted a continuous flow of visitors, many of whom were entertained with food and lodging. The midden that reflects this principal episode of occupation is more extensive than any reported on-island, suggesting a long, intensive period of formation; the likely recipient of the by-products of both entertainment and production systems. Canoes were coming and going from the site; a vigorous trade in a variety of goods is suggested in the size and extent of the off-loading zone adjacent to the main canoe landing, as well as the manufacturing debitage within the site itself; medicine may have been one of the commodities controlled by site residents (such facilities are not present in other sites around this part of the island); and the presence of a formal entrance marked by coral rounds indicates a degree of pomp and ceremony not present at any other nearby site.

Sometime during the 17th century, Safonfok was abandoned. Occupation dwindled to the point where little, if any, evidence of use remained. Even memories of Safonfok as one of the principal power brokers during the formative, pre-Leluh era seems to have disappeared. For all intents and purposes, Safonfok as a living site and administrative center ceased to exist. Political maneuverings on the other side of the island were underway. Within a century, the meteoric rise of Leluh would mark a new era on the island—one of unification under the tyrannical thumb of a single, paramount ruler.

By the time the western explorers arrived, Safonfok as a place name (let alone an ancient residential site of high chiefs) was unknown—the earliest European explorers failed to list it among the inhabited or formerly inhabited regions of the island. With the arrival of missionaries and establishment of the Mwot Mission, Safonfok became a convenient but temporary camp for a shipwrecked Marshallese family that needed close quarters to the mission. It also became the hunting grounds for Mission students in search of land crabs. And then, sometime during the last century or so, a plantation of breadfruit and coconuts were planted within the compound. The young plants thrived on the nutritionally enriched midden deposits, setting down a web of roots that engulfed and further mixed this matrix. These young plants matured, along with their roots, which have proven to be a major obstacle in our excavations. The surrounding community too further contributed to the gradual dismantlement of the site. To them, the site was a good source of building materials, so they scavenged portions of the wall.

Today, Safonfok stands abandoned, nearly hidden in a thick jungled strand vegetation. It was once thought to be heavily disturbed because the surrounding wall had collapsed and structural foundations had shifted and were partially buried with little surface indication of their presence remaining. About the only visitors to the site have been pigs and land crabs, both of which are now considered the primary agents of destruction. Then came the archaeologists. After two seasons of intensive archaeological investigations, Safonfok was transformed into one of the most unique sites on the island and in the Pacific. Coral fishhooks and their supporting manufacturing industry were recovered here, propelling the site into yet another unanticipated role: that of *type site*, the place where an artifact type new to the archaeological record is recognized and described. Archaeological investigations also demonstrated that the site, contrary to its surface conditions, contains a relatively intact subsurface deposit that is likely to yield a great deal more information on the activities within the site

When the archaeologists left, the pigs and land crabs resumed their grubbing and burrowing. They are simply agents in a never-ending cycle of disruption, disturbance and decay. Every day Nature and her fury act to undermine the site, its structural presence, and even its buried strata. Further cultural damage, the by-product of human activity, is at least ameliorated, with Safonfok sheltered by the Kosrae legal code, a growing sense of 'pride in place' being expressed across the island, and even its increased visibility as a significant component in the archaeological record of the island and region.

## *Project Objectives*

With only 0.3% of the site excavated, we have already been able to fill in some of the activities and probable events that took place during the formative era of Kosrae's traditional prehistory. And, we recovered a technological industry—coral fishhooks—that has never been reported or documented in the archaeological record of the Pacific. Both of these accomplishments went well beyond the project objectives set forward during the planning stages for the archaeological investigation of Safonfok. In their original form, project objectives (expressed as research themes or issues) were intended to address very basic archaeological tasks, such as establishment of a local chronology, patterns of material consumption, and a continuing inquiry into settlement patterns and site types. The end result, however, was something that could not have been predicted, but which proved a boon to archaeological research on the island—the tangible recovery of a rich assemblage of new data and new insights into a part of the past that has received little attention in the overall history of archaeological exploration on the island.

### Chronology

Several radiocarbon dates were derived from charcoal and shell samples systematically recovered throughout the excavations. The dates place Safonfok squarely in the formative, pre-Leluh era of Kosrae's traditional history, a time of increasing complexity when autonomous regional centers were jockeying for power, status and position. Initial occupation at Safonfok appears to have occurred some time before A.D. 1200; the presence of a single buried coral pavement provides mute testimony to this occupation. After A.D. 1200, there is a rapid growth in population within the site area, along with a more intensive use of the site, increasing resource exploitation, and a growing political complexity that peaked between A.D. 1400 and 1600. At the height of its administrative glory, Safonfok was a presence to be respected and perhaps feared. It was strategically located, controlled certain precious commodities and the industries that produced them, and maintained control over at least one segment of the island and its adjoining lagoon.

By the 18th century, Safonfok was virtually abandoned and forgotten—so far, no oral histories recount families, deeds, or other actions associated with the traditional occupation of the site. Safonfok does not seem to have a history, at least not a traditional oral history. During the 19th and early 20th centuries, according to local stories, the site was briefly occupied by a Marshallese family attached to the nearby Mwot Mission. Thereafter, Safonfok became a source for building materials, land crabs and other commodities.

In addition to radiocarbon dates, stratigraphic sequences and oral histories reaffirm and confirm the scientifically derived chronometric dates.

## Material Culture

Among the secrets slowly revealed by the Safonfok deposits was a wealth of information on production industries. Residues of coral fishhook manufacture, adze production, canoe construction and even the remnants of bead production—all are present within the Safonfok midden, including scattered fragments of raw materials, articles under production or broken during production, tools, and discarded items that had exhausted their use-life. Just the presence of the full complement of even one industry would have made Safonfok an unusual site in the inventory of Kosrae sites; Safonfok, however, has more than one industry contained in its deposits, all of which consist of the full complement of workmanship—from raw material testing to finished products to discard. Until Safonfok, much of our current knowledge about traditional technologies was drawn from ethnohistorical observations and archaeological accounts of other Micronesian high islands.

The appearance of coral fishhooks in the site inventory has propelled Safonfok into the position of *type site*. Physical examples of these hooks have never been recovered before in the archaeological record of Kosrae, the region or the Pacific. Their occurrence in fishing industries of the past (specifically, in Tuvalu) have been reported, although often accompanied with the qualifier that these are very ancient hooks no longer exist and have not been seen for generations. Coral fishhooks and their range of variation are described from the specimens recovered at Safonfok.

Safonfok provides a window into traditional cultural practices of the past, while at the same time reinforces another more general observation regarding the likely origin of Kosrae culture—that it was derived from low coral islands, where marine resources provided the majority of raw materials. The archaeological inventory at Safonfok demonstrates a predilection toward marine resources, with minimal use of stone and other terrestrial materials.

## Pottery

No pottery was observed or recovered at Safonfok.

## Settlement Pattern

Safonfok's contribution to settlement pattern studies on Kosrae is in the recognition of a series of large self-contained sites in existence during the formative era. All are coastal sites occupying strategic locations defined by natural features such as rivers, embayments, ridges, and even clifflines. The formative era, it seems, has become one of active political competition with an economic network focused on items of prestige and utility. Until excavations at Safonfok, this active, highly competitive formative era in Kosrae's history was routinely dismissed. It was frequently described, without benefit of label, as a quaint period of small but autonomous centers bumbling through their existence in search of a leader. The site of Leluh answered that call, unified the island and became the focal point of a paramountcy that would rule the island with an iron fist.

Architecturally, Safonfok exhibits an overall plan and style of construction that is prelude to Leluh, the architectural end-point in the traditional record of Kosrae. Safonfok, for instance, makes light use of basalt as a wall veneer; by the time Leluh is constructed, this veneer will become much more massive and serve as the defining feature of all subsequent architectural endeavors. Safonfok also has reinforced openings through its surrounding compound wall (the structural foundations of which can be seen in the rubble of the collapsed walls); multiple openings, including at least one formal entry; and at least two canoe ramps, one formal and one informal. In short, a differential pattern of status and rank is already built into the site; visually, Safonfok is a symbol of class differences—high versus low, chief versus commoner, master versus servant. These divisions will become more distinct as Leluh rises to power, with class differences heavily exploited by the time western explorers set foot on the island.

What has not changed—whether in Safonfok, in other formative era sites, or even in the later Leluh—is the dispersed settlement pattern common to low islands. Individual compounds continue to house extended families, with high status compounds containing multiple structures within its walls, often with its associated populations (servants, artisans) settling just beyond the outer walls. High status structures tend to exhibit more substantial construction techniques, often built with materials that survive time; whereas, low status households and structures tend to be raised with perishable materials, with only the residues of daily life remaining in the preservable record as evidence of their existence.

## Increased Complexity

The size, features and artifact content of Safonfok directly address its role as a powerful center during the formative, pre-Leluh era of Kosrae's history. It was a wealthy site in a number of ways—first and foremost, it displayed monumentality and an appreciation for aesthetics in architectural design; it controlled production industries and other proprietary knowledge (such as medicine); it received and entertained foreign (outside its landed boundaries) dignitaries; it was a center for economic activity; and it retained the services of a local community that existed just outside its walls.

During the formative era, a number of powerful administrative centers were negotiating for power, status and control over resources. Safonfok was one of a few large complexes distributed around the coastline; others within this same class of sites include Likinlulem, Lacl, Nefalil, and Yacl. All appear to be autonomous administrative centers, more than likely with designs for greater territorial domination. Yet, none ultimately prevailed. Leluh's meteoric rise on the opposite side of the island trumped them all and soon became the center of the paramountcy. Places like Safonfok and Likinlulem very quickly became insignificant, abandoned and, in the case of Safonfok, forgotten.

### Subsistence

Faunal analyses are still underway, although some observations are applicable. Bivalves, for example, appear to dominate the midden deposit throughout Safonfok. According to Athens (1995), there was an early emphasis on bivalve exploitation in the archaeological record of Kosrae, with a gradual but visible decline after A.D. 500, when gastropods came to dominate the shellfish record. While the dates for Safonfok do not reflect the early, A.D. 500 time frame, the dominance of bivalves may indicate their prevalence in in-shore waters and a rich marine environment rather than a chronological association.

### Environment

Together, the stratigraphic profiles across Safonfok suggest a generalized geological history for this part of the coastline. It was one that began in an unknown, undated era with an active beach in the place of Safonfok. As the shoreline prograded, building lagoonward, a back-beach deposit began to develop. The timing for this event is again unknown, although estimated to be some time before A.D. 1200. A leveled coral pavement spanning the active and back-beach deposits was put in place at about this time.

The shoreline continued to prograde, while the back-beach deposit continued to develop. The leveled pavement was soon buried while a coastal strand vegetation established itself on the back-beach; rootlets and the residues of vegetation patterns remain visible in the sediments. At the same time, Safonfok as a site was raised in a more substantial form than the previous pavement. This took place after A.D. 1200 and continued throughout the formative era. Use and eventual abandonment of the site did not alter the ever-continuous process of shoreline progradation, back-beach development and vegetation growth, expansion and regrowth. Human contributions to the vegetation community include medicinal plants, several different food plants, and both decorative and utilitarian plants.

Adjacent to Safonfok is a mangrove channel that serves as the principal avenue of access into and out of the site. When and under what conditions the mangrove channel was carved into the landscape remains unknown, although its presence during the initial settlement and throughout the use of Safonfok is likely. Athens (1995) suggests the period between A.D. 1100 and 1300 provided ideal conditions for the growth and expansion of mangrove forests (and by extension, channels). This was a time when falling sea levels reached their modern levels, which reduced water circulation in the lagoon that in turn created favorable habitat for mangrove development.

## Significance

One of the overall tasks of project work was to assess the significance of Safonfok relative to the U.S. National Register of Historic Places criteria. Significance is measured against a scale of eligibility criteria, each of which describes a broad area in the pattern of human accomplishments in the past. For an historical (archaeological) site to be considered significant, it must have above all integrity—a preserved entity that is intact and *in situ*—and it must meet at least one of four kinds of connections to the past:

A. Association with the lives of persons significant in the past;

B. Association with events that have made a significant contribution to the broad pattern of history;

C. Embody distinctive characteristics of a type, period, or methods of construction, or retain characteristics that represent the works of a master, possess high artistic value, or represent a significant and distinguishable entity whose components may lack individual distinctions; or,

D. Have yielded, or may be likely to yield, information significant to history or prehistory.

For Safonfok, only Criterion D is applicable. Colloquially, Criterion D is referred to as the scientific data category, the one category that can accommodate archaeological sites and prehistoric deposits where little additional information is available regarding the historical conditions and events that led to the formation of the archaeological record. According to National Register Bulletin 15, in order to meet requirements for a determination of significance under Criterion D, a site must: a) be evaluated within the appropriate context, b) demonstrate a connection with research questions derived from the academic community or pertinent preservation programs, c) establish the presence of adequate data, d) possess informational integrity, e) have the potential to yield important information with the remaining portions, unless f) the site retains the ability to convey its association as the former repository of important information, the location of historic events, or is the representative of important trends (USDI 1991).

By all accounts, Safonfok is most definitely a site that has yielded and has the potential of yielding additional information important and significant to the occupation history of Kosrae, of the region, and in the Pacific. Yes, it has, over time, been the recipient of several levels of disturbance, both cultural and natural. Yet, it still retains sufficient data, sufficient structure, informational value and research potential to address questions of local and regional prehistory, as well as to contribute to the very fabric of the archaeological record in the Pacific (and beyond). The quality and composition of some of the physical properties of the site have suffered—the surrounding wall is collapsed and disassembled, structural foundations appear disjointed and distorted, portions of the subsurface deposit have been mixed through the agents of rooting pigs and burrowing crabs— yet, in spite of this, Safonfok and its contents have not been diminished. The site still retains a wealth of materials, intact deposits and deposits thicker than have ever been encountered in previous archaeological sites investigated on island; the site, in other words, embodies values that stimulate curious and tempered imaginations, and exhibits a degree of integrity unexpected given the state of its surface condition.

Safonfok too has become a *type site* for coral fishhooks, an artifact type that is new to the archaeological record of the island, the region and the Pacific. It is the first archaeological site in the Pacific in which coral fishhooks have been observed, physically recovered and reported. Two earlier accounts of coral fishhooks exist in the archaeological literature of the Pacific; however, both recount oral testimony that recalls such ancient and primitive apparatus (Hedley 1896, Beasley 1928), but neither report actual physical specimens of these fishhooks. In 2002, I recovered coral fishhooks from archaeological deposits on Kwajalein Atoll, in the Marshall Islands; however, had it not been for the precedent established at Safonfok, outlining their very existence and variety of forms, I find myself questioning whether I would have been able to identify the specimens on Kwajalein as fishhooks.

For the history of Kosrae, Safonfok provides a record of continuity, duration and cultural complexity in the formative era of Kosrae's occupational history. In fact, it was an established presence during this era, and appears to have been one of the power brokers of the time, wielding control over the production of precious commodities such as canoes, adzes and beads, while at the same time taking part in an island-wide struggle for political and economic power, position, and status. From the standpoint of the U.S. National Register, Safonfok has and will continue to supply invaluable information on questions of social, political and economic organization within a period of time that is not well understood. It can also offer insights into settlement patterns, local and regional resource exploitation, and even the nature of post-depositional processes that affect site formation and alteration over time. Granted, these are but a very few topics out of a much wider range of possible topics that can be addressed. In the broader context, they are simply illustrative of the capacity of Safonfok to meaningfully contribute to our understanding of the web of life and activity that once dominated the island.

## Some Concluding Remarks

On 17 February 2002, Safonfok was entered onto the U.S. National Register of Historic Places. This was a defining moment for the site, as it represented a recognition of Safonfok's unique qualities by others beyond the shores of Kosrae. It was also a move that could not have been predicted during the first days of archaeological investigations. But, looking back on the excavations, with fieldwork completed and sufficient time having elapsed to contemplate overall results in a more philosophical light, the Safonfok project was an unexpected, unqualified success. What started as a training exercise in a site described as heavily disturbed produced one of the more significant sites on the island, in the region, and in the Pacific. In the history of archaeological research, new artifact types and the sites from which they are initially defined—*type sites*—are few in number; so few, in fact, that they rarely appear in the literature. As an archaeologist, you never expect to encounter such a beast, perhaps because of a general complacency and agreement-by-default that any 'new' artifacts are most likely to be variations on an existing theme. Yet here at Safonfok, the new artifacts—coral fishhooks—did not fit that pattern. They really were new to the archaeological record, or rather, they were the first physical specimens to enter the archaeological record; the literature had already reported such hooks but with the caveat that they were so ancient no examples had been seen for generations. Safonfok produced the first tangible examples of these fishhooks.

Safonfok too displayed a broad range of technologies that defined the material culture complex of traditional, pre-Leluh Kosrae, the island's formative era. Here again, Safonfok surprised the excavation team, who expected (at least initially) even the subsurface component of the site to parallel the disturbance seen on the surface. Afterall, this was a site routinely scavenged for building materials by local residents; where pigs rooted, crabs burrowed and a thick cover of jungle just got thicker. Yet, below the surface, the site was transformed. The full complement of a wide variety of manufacturing industries was present and heavily distributed throughout the site matrix—raw materials, tools, the items themselves in various stages of completion and discard— along with a thick, black, intact midden deposit that once more was without precedence in the archaeological inventory of Kosrae.

In virtually every aspect of recovery, Safonfok not only met but surpassed expectations.  For Kosrae, our efforts demonstrated that disturbed sites cannot be so easily dismissed; that they may in fact contain significant information that not only contributes to local and regional histories, but can securely delineate a major episode in the development of the island's political and social complexity.   As part of a growing complex of formative, pre-Leluh sites, Safonfok has elevated the need to understand and chart the roots of later eras.  The power and status of Leluh, for example, is no longer an aberration in the political history Kosrae, nor is it the result of outside forces subjugating small, passive but autonomous chiefdoms that occupied the island.  It was instead the by-product of a much more animated history of conflict, alliance-building, and posturing for power, prestige and control.

Safonfok has, in essence, served as a catalyst for restructuring the past and defining the formative pre-Leluh era.  It should also serve as a beacon for others to take note of the range of possible traditional technologies that can occur at a single site, as well as a clarion call to employ at all times a tempered imagination when drawing connections between disparate pieces of information to produce a holistic interpretation of the site and its context in time and space.  Safonfok is not the first site on Kosrae to be systematically examined and excavated, nor will it be the last.   However, the excavation of Safonfok will most certainly influence future archaeological investigations.   With a more substantial chronological foundation now delimited, such future endeavors have but to reap greater rewards in an unhindered flow of information relating past to present.

# REFERENCES

Allen, J.A., K.C. Ewel and J. Jack
2001    Patterns of Natural and Anthropogenic Disturbance of the Mangroves on the Pacific Island of Kosrae. *Wetlands Ecology and Management* 9: 291-301.

Anell, Bengt
1955    *Contribution to the History of Fishing in the Southern Seas*. Studia Ethnographica Upsaliensea IX, Uppsala.

Ashby, Gene, editor
1989    *Never and Always: Micronesian Legends, Fables and Folklore, by the Students of the Community College of Micronesia*. Rainy Day Press, Pohnpei, FSM and Eugene, Oregon.

Athens, J. Stephen
1986    *Archaeological Investigations at Tarague Beach, Guam*. International Archaeological Institute, Inc., Honolulu.

1990    Kosrae Pottery, Clay, and Early Settlement. *Micronesica* Supplement 2: 171-186.

1995    *Landscape Archaeology: Prehistoric Settlement, Subsistence, and Environment of Kosrae, Eastern Caroline Islands, Micronesia*. International Archaeological Institute, Inc., Honolulu.

Athens, J. Stephen, Ross Cordy, K. Shun, Charles F. Streck, and Takeshi Ueki
1983    *Kosrae Circumferential Road Survey: Archaeological Site Descriptions and Test Excavations*. Draft report for the Office of Historic Preservation, U.S. Trust Territory of the Pacific Islands, Saipan.

Barerra, W.M., Jr. and P.V. Kirch
1973    Basaltic Glass Artifacts from Hawai'i: Their Dating and Prehistoric Uses. *Journal of the Polynesian Society* 82(2): 176-187.

Bath, Joyce E.
1986    *Archaeological Salvage on Water Lines B and D, Lelu, Kosrae*. Report for the Kosrae Office of History and Culture, Kosrae.

Bath, Joyce E. and Kanalei Shun
1982    *Archaeological Salvage on Water Line C, Lelu, Kosrae*. Report for the Kosrae Office of History and Culture, Kosrae.

Bath, Joyce E., Kanalei Shun and Ross Cordy
1983    *Archaeological Investigations at Likhnhluhlwem and Leahp (the Kosrae Phase 2 Project)*. Report for the Kosrae Office of History and Culture, Kosrae.

Beardsley, Felicia R.
1994    *Archaeological Investigations on Kwajalein Atoll, Marshall Islands*. International Archaeological Research Institute, Inc., Honolulu.

1996    *Fragments of Paradise: Archaeological Investigations in the Republic of Palau*. International Archaeological Research Institute, Inc., Honolulu, Hawaii.

1997a    Fishponds, Taro Patches and Shell Middens: Archaeological Investigations on Peleliu, Republic of Palau, Data Recovery and Monitoring for the Palau Rural Water System Program. International Archaeological Research Institute, Inc., Honolulu, Hawaii.

1997b    Pacific Islands Collection at the University of California, Riverside's California Museum of Photography (UCR CMP). *Journal of Pacific Studies*, vol. 20, nr 4, special issue on photography.

Beasley, H.G.
1928    *Pacific Islands Records: Fish Hooks*. Seely, Service and Co., Ltd., London.

Bell, J.A.
1994    *Reconstructing Prehistory: Scientific Methods in Archaeology*. Temple University Press, Philadelphia.

Bernart, Luelen
1977    *The Book of Luelen*, translated by J.L. Fischer, S.H. Riesenberg and M.G. Whiting. Australian National University Press, Canberra.

Boas, Franz
1929    *The Mind of Primitive Man*. The Macmillan Company, New York

Borofsky, Robert, ed.
2000    *Remembrance of Pacific Pasts: An Invitation to Remake History*. University of Hawai'i Press, Honolulu.

Bronowski, Jacob
1978    *The Visionary Eye: Essays in the Arts, Literature, and Sciences*. The MIT Press, Cambridge, Massachusetts.

Buck, P.H. (Te Rangi Hiroa)
1957    *Death and Burial: Arts and Crafts of Hawai'i.*
B.P. Bishop Museum Special Publication 45. Bernice P.
Bishop Museum, Honolulu.

Buddemeier, R.W., S.V. Smith and R.A. Kinzie
1975    Holocene Windward Reef-flat History,
Enewetak Atoll. *Geological Society of America Bulletin*
86: 1581-1584.

Butler, B.
1988    *Archaeological Investigations on the North
Coast of Rota, Mariana Islands.* Micronesian
Archaeological Survey , Report 23. Southern Illinois
University, Center for Archaeological Investigations,
Occasional Paper Nr. 8, Carbondale.

Christian, F. W.
1899    *The Caroline Islands.* Charles Scribner's Sons,
New York.

Cole. T.G., K.C. Ewel and N.N. Devoe
1999    Structure of Mangrove Trees and Forests in
Micronesia. *Forest Ecology and Management* 117: 95-
109.

Cordy, Ross
1981    *Archaeological Investigations in Wiya and
Tepat Fal, Kosrae.* Historic Preservation Office, U.S.
Trust Territory of the Pacific Islands, Saipan.

1982a    Lelu, The Stone City of Kosrae: 1978 -1981
Research. *Journal of the Polynesian Society* 91(1): 103-
119.

1982b    Archaeological Research on Kosrae (Eastern
Caroline Islands). *Bulletin of the Indo-Pacific Prehistory
Association* 3: 129-134.

1985    Investigations of Leluh's Stone Ruins. *National
Geographic Research* 1: 255-263.

1993    *The Lelu Stone Ruins (Kosrae, Micronesia):
1978-81 Historical and Archaeological Research.* Asian
and Pacific Series Nr. 10, Social Science Research
Institute, University of Hawaii. University of Hawaii
Press, Honolulu.

Cordy, Ross, ed.
1983    *Archaeological Survey of Innem, Okat, and
Loa!, Kosrae Island.* Micronesian Archaeological
Survey Report Nr. 7. Historic Preservation Office, U.S.
Trust Territory of the Pacific Islands, Saipan.

Cordy, Ross, Joyce Bath, Kanalei Shun and J. Stephen
Athens
1985    *Archaeological Data Recovery in Central Utwa,
Kosrae Circumferential Road.* Kosrae Office of History
and Culture, Kosrae.

Cordy, Ross and Takeshi Ueki
1983    The Development of Complex Societies on
Kosrae. Paper presented at the annual meeting of the
Society for American Archaeology, Pittsburgh,
Pennsylvania.

Craib, John
1977    *A Typological Investigation of Western
Micronesian Adzes.* M.A. Thesis, California State
University, Long Beach.

1978    *Archaeological Reconnaissance Survey on
Kosrae for the Kosrae Airport-Harbor Project.* Historic
Preservation Office, U.S. Trust Territory of the Pacific
Islands, Saipan.

1989    *Archaeological Reconnaissance Survey and
Sampling: U.S. Army Kwajalein Atoll Facility (USAKA),
Kwajalein Atoll, Republic of the Marshall Islands,
Micronesia.* Report prepared for U.S. Army Engineer
District, Pacific Ocean Division, Fort Shafter, Hawaii.

Devoe, N.N.
1994    Mangrove Exploitation and Conservation in the
Federated States of Micronesia. *Isla: A Journal of
Micronesian Studies* 2:1 (Rainy Season): 67-82.

Devoe, N.N. and T.G. Cole
1998    Growth and Yield in Mangrove Forests of the
Federated States of Micronesia. *Forest Ecology and
Management* 103: 33-48.

Drexler, J.Z. and K.C. Ewel
2001    Effects of ENSO-Related Drought on
Hydrology and Salinity in a Micronesian Wetland
Complex. *Estuaries* 24: 347-356.

Duff, R.
1970    *Stone Adzes of Southeast Asia.* Canterbury
Museum Bulletin 3, Christchurch.

Dye, Tom
1987    Introduction. *Marshall Islands Archaeology,*
ed. by T. Dye, pp. 1-16. Pacific Anthropological
Records Nr. 38, Bernice P. Bishop Museum, Honolulu.

Emory, K.P., W.J. Bonk and Y.H. Sinoto
1959    *Fishhooks.* Bernice P. Bishop Museum Special
Publication 47, Bishop Museum Press, Honolulu.

Ewel, K.C., J.A. Bourgeois, T.G. Cole and S. Zheng
1998    Variation in Environmental Characteristics and Vegetation in High-Rainfall Mangrove Swamps in Kosrae, Micronesia. *Global Ecology and Biogeography Letters* 7: 49-56.

Ewel, K.C., R.R. Twilley and J.E. Ong
1998    Different Kinds of Mangrove Forests Provide Different Goods and Services. *Global Ecology and Biogeography Letters* 7: 83-94.

Favreau, C.K.
1993    Appendix B: Analysis of Shell and Basalt Adzes from the Leo Palace Hotel Site. *Archaeological Investigations at the Leo Palace Site, Naton, Tumon Bay, Guam, Vo. 1: Archaeological Data Recovery, Burial Recovery, and Monitorying*, ed. by B.D. Davis, M.J. Tomonari-Tuggle and S. Wickler. International Archaeological Research Institute, Inc., Honolulu.

1995    Non-Ceramic Portable Artifacts. *Landscape Archaeology: Prehistoric Settlement, Subsistence, and Environment of Kosrae, Eastern Caroline Islands, Micronesia*, S. Athens, pp. 277-298. International Archaeological Institute, Inc., Honolulu.

Graves, M.W.
1986    Late Prehistoric Complexity on Lelu: Alternatives to Cordy's Model. *Journal of the Polynesian Society* 95: 479-489.

Green, R.C.
1974    A Review of Portable Artifacts from Western Samoa. *Archaeology in Western Samoa, Vol. II.* Bulletin of the Auckland Institute and Museum 7, Auckland.

Hedley, C.
1896    General Account of Funafuti Atoll. *The Atoll of Funafuti, Ellice Group: Its Zoology, Botany, Ethnology and General Structure.* Australian Msueum, Sydney.

Hunter-Anderson, Rosalind L.
2002    From Palau to Rapanui, Are the Pacific Island Grasslands Recent "Artifacts" or Natural Formations? *Bulletin of the Indo-Pacific Prehistory Association* [in press]

Intoh, Michiko
1986    Pigs in Micronesia:  Introduction or Re-introduction by the Europeans? *Man and Culture in Oceania* 2: 1-26.

1996    Multi-Regional Contacts of Prehistoric Fais Islanders in Micronesia. *Indo-Pacific Prehistory Association Bulletin 15: Chiang Mai Papers* Vol. 2, pp. 111-117.

Johannes, R.E.
1981    *Words of the Lagoon: Fishing and Marine Lore in the Palau District of Micronesia.* University of California Press, Berkeley.

Kirch, P.V.
1979    *Marine Exploitation in Prehistoric Hawai'i: Archaeological Investigations at Kalahuipua'a, Hawai'i Island.* Pacific Anthropological Records Nr. 29, Bernice P. Bishop Museum, Honolulu.

Kirch, P.V. and D.E. Yen
1982    *Tikopia: The Prehistory and Ecology of a Polynesian Outlier.* B.P. Bishop Museum Bulletin 238. Bishop Museum Press, Honolulu.

Malinowski, B.
1984    *Argonauts of the Western Pacific: An Account of Native Enterprise and Adventure in the Archipelagoes of Melanesian New Guinea.* Waveland Press, Prospect Heights, Illinois [originally published in 1922]

Masse, W. Bruce, David Snyder and George J. Gumerman
1984    Prehistoric and Historic Settlement in the Palau Islands, Micronesia. *New Zealand Journal of Archaeology* 6: 107-127.

Maude, Henry Evans and R.J. Lampert
1967    The Stalactite Fish Hooks of Ocean Island. *Journal of the Polynesian Society* 76(4): 415-125.

Moir, B.G.
1986-87 A Review of Tridacnid Ecology and Some possible Implications for Archaeological Research. *Asian Perspectives* 27(1): 95-121.

Morgan, William N.
1988    *Prehistoric Architecture in Micronesia.* University of Texas Press, Austin.

Naylor, R. and M. Drew
1998    Valuing Mangrove Resources in Kosrae, Micronesia. *Environment and Development Economics* 3: 471-490.

Nunn, Patrick D.
1994    *Oceanic Islands.* Blackwell Publishers, Oxford, UK and Cambridge, USA.

Osborne, Douglas
1966    *The Archaeology of the Palau Islands, an Intensive Survey.* Bernice P. Bishop Museum Bulletin 230, Honolulu.

1979    *Archaeological Test Excavations, Palau Islands, 1968-1969.* Micronesica Supplement 1.

Parmentier, Richard J.
1987 *The Sacred Remains: Myth, History, and Polity in Belau.* University of Chicago Press, Chicago and London.

Reeve, R.
1989 Recent Work on the Prehistory of the Western Solomons, Melanesia. Indo-Pacific Prehistory Association Bulletin9: 44-67.

Richardson, J.M.
1993 A Practical Guide to Field Sampling for Geological Problems. *Analysis of Geological Materials*, ed. by C. Riddle, pp. 37-64. Marcel Dekker, Inc., Hong Kong.

Riley, T.J.
1987 Archaeological Survey and Testing, Majuro Atoll, Marshall Islands. *Marshall Islands Archaeology*, ed. by T. Dye, pp. 169-270. Pacific Anthropological Records Nr. 38, Bernice P. Bishop Museum, Honolulu.

Ritter, Lynn Takata and Philip L. Ritter
1982 *The European Discovery of Kosrae Island: Accounts by Louis Isidore Duperrey, Jules Sebastien Cesar Dumont D'Urville, Rene Primevere Lesson, Fyedor Lutke, and Friedrich Heinrich von Kittlitz.* Micronesian Archaeological Survey Report Nr. 13. Historic Preservation Office, U.S. Trust Territory of the Pacific Islands, Saipan.

Rosendahl, P.H.
1987 Archaeology in Eastern Micronesia: Reconnaissance Survey in the Marshall Islands. *Marshall Islands Archaeology*, ed. by T. Dye, pp. 17-168. Pacific Anthropological Records Nr. 38, Bernice P. Bishop Museum, Honolulu.

Sarfert, Ernst
1919 *Kosrae. Vol. 1, Ethnography: General Information and Material Culture. Results of the South Seas Expedition 1908-1910.* L. Friederichsen, de Gruyter & Co., Hamburg [tranlated by E.A. Murphy, 1983]

1920 *Kosrae. Vol. 2. Non-Material Culture. Results of the South Seas Expedition 1908-1910.* L. Friederichsen, de Gruyter & Co., Hamburg [tranlated by E.A. Murphy, 1983]

Sakamoto, Izumi
1994 Study of Geological Characteristics of Volcanic Rocks from Kosrae Island, Eastern Caroline Islands. *Journal of the Faculty of Marine Science and Technology.* Tokai University, Japan.

Shun, Kanalei and J.Stephen Athens
1990 Archaeological Investigations on Kwajalein Atoll, Marshall Islands, Micronesia. *Micronesica* Supplement 2: 231-240.

Shutler, Richard, Jr.
1984 Description of Pottery from Sites TKFE-2, -3, -4, -5. *Caroline Islands Archaeology: Investigations on Fefan, Faraulep, Woleai, and Lamotrek*, ed. by Sinoto, pp. 44-53. Pacific Anthropological Records Nr. 35, Bernice P. Bishop Museum, Honolulu.

Sinoto, Yosihiko
1979 Coding System for Hawaiian Fishhooks. *Marine Exploitation in Prehistoric Hawai'i: Archaeological Investigations at Kalahuipua'a, Hawai'i Island*, by P.V. Kirch, pp. 231-233. Pacific Anthropological Records Nr. 29, Bernice P. Bishop Museum, Honolulu.

1982 *Report on the Test Excavation of the Bird Cave, Site D-16, on Kosrae Island, East Caroline Islands.* Bernice P. Bishop Museum, Honolulu.

Spoehr, A.
1957 *Marianas Prehistory: Archaeological Survey and Excavations on Saipan, Tinian and Rota.* Fieldiana: Anthropology, Vol. 48, Chicago Natural History Museum.

Streck, C., Jr.
1990 Prehistoric Settlement in Eastern Micronesia: Archaeology on Bikini Atoll, Republic of the Marshall Islands. *Micronesica* Supplement 2: 247-260.

Swift, Marilyn K., Randy A. Harper and J. Stephen Athens
1990 *Studies in the Prehistory of Malem Municipality: Kosrae Archaeology, Miconesian Resources Study.* Micronesian Endowment for Historic Preservation, F.S.M. Historic Preservation Office, Pohnpei. International Archaeological Research Institute, Inc., Honolulu.

Trigger, B.
1989 *A History of Archaeological Thought.* Cambridge University Press, Cambridge.

U.S. Department of Agriculture, Soil Conservation Service
1983 *Soil Survey of the Island of Kosrae, Federated States of Micronesia.* National Cooperative Soil Survey, U.S. Department of Argiculture, Washington, D.C.

U.S. Department of the Interior, National Park Service
1991 *How to Apply the National Register Criteria for Evaluation.* Bulletin 15, National Register of History

Places, U.S. Department of the Interior, Washington, D.C.

Wallace, Alfred Russel
1962    *The Malay Archipelago.*  Dover Publications, Inc., New York [first published 1869 by Macmillan and Company, London]

Weisler, Marshall I.
2001    *On the Margins of Sustainability: Prehistoric Settlement of Utrok Atoll, Northern Marshalls Islands.* BAR International Series 967, BAR Publishing, Oxford.

Welch, David J., Judith R. McNeill and J. Stephen Athens
1990    *Intensive Archaeological Survey of the RS-3 Circumferential Road Corridor, Okat Valley, Kosrae, Eastern Caroline Islands, Micronesia.* International Archaeological Research Institute, Inc., Honolulu.

Wheeler, Sir Mortimer
1955    *Archaeology from the Earth.*  Clarendon Press, Oxford.

Willey, Gordon R., A. Ledyard Smith, Gair Tourtellot III, Ian Graham
1975    Report 1, Introduction:  the Site and Its Setting. *Excavations at Seibal, Department of Peten, Guatemala.*

Peabody Museum of Archaeology and Ethnology, Harvard University, Cambridge.

Willey, G.R. and J.A. Sabloff
1980    *A History of American Archaeology.*  W.H. Freeman, San Francisco.
Yawata, Ichiro
1930    The Fish-Shaped Fishhooks in Micronesia. *Zinruigaku Zasshi* 45(4) [english translation available at Bishop Museum, Honolulu]

1932a    Hidden Treasure in the Excavations. *Dorumen* 1:15-18 [english translation by P. Chapman, 1964: *Micronesian Archaeology: An Annotated Bibliography*, M.A. Thesis, Stanford University]

1932b    On the Megalithic Structures of Kusaie and Ponape.  *Chirigaku Hyooron* 8(4): 310-326 [english translation by P. Chapman]

Young, L.B.
1999    *Islands: Portraits of Miniature Worlds.*  W.H. Freeman and Company, New York.

ADDENDUM:

RADIOCARBON DATES AND CALIBRATIONS

# The University of Waikato
## Radiocarbon Dating Laboratory

Private Bag 3105
Hamilton,
New Zealand.
Fax +64 7 838 4192
Ph +64 7 838 4278
email c14@waikato.ac.nz
Head: Dr Alan Hogg

## Report on Radiocarbon Age Determination for Wk-     9475

| | |
|---|---|
| **Submitter** | F Beardsley |
| **Submitter's Code** | 29 Unit 2/3 hearth |
| **Site & Location** | Safonfok, Kosrae, Fed States Micronesia, Micronesia |
| **Sample Material** | Charcoal |
| **Physical Pretreatment** | Possible contaminants were removed. |
| **Chemical Pretreatment** | Sample washed in hot 10% HCl, rinsed and treated with hot 2% NaOH. The NaOH insoluble fraction was treated with hot 10% HCl, filtered, rinsed and dried. |

| | | |
|---|---|---|
| $d^{14}C$ | -39.6 ± 5.7 | ‰ |
| $\delta^{13}C$ | -26.2 ± 0.2 | ‰ |
| $D^{14}C$ | -37.3 ± 7.0 | ‰ |
| % Modern | 96.3 ± 0.7 | % |
| **Result** | **306 ± 58 BP** | |

## Comments

*AHHogg*
8/6/01

- Result is *Conventional Age or % Modern* as per Stuiver and Polach, 1977, Radiocarbon 19, 355-363. This is based on the Libby half-life of 5568 yr with correction for isotopic fractionation applied. This age is normally quoted in publications and must include the appropriate error term and Wk number.

- Quoted errors are 1 standard deviation due to counting statistics multiplied by an experimentally determined Laboratory Error Multiplier of 1.217 .

- The isotopic fractionation, $\delta^{13}C$, is expressed as ‰ wrt PDB.

- Results are reported as % *Modern* when the conventional age is younger than 200 yr BP.

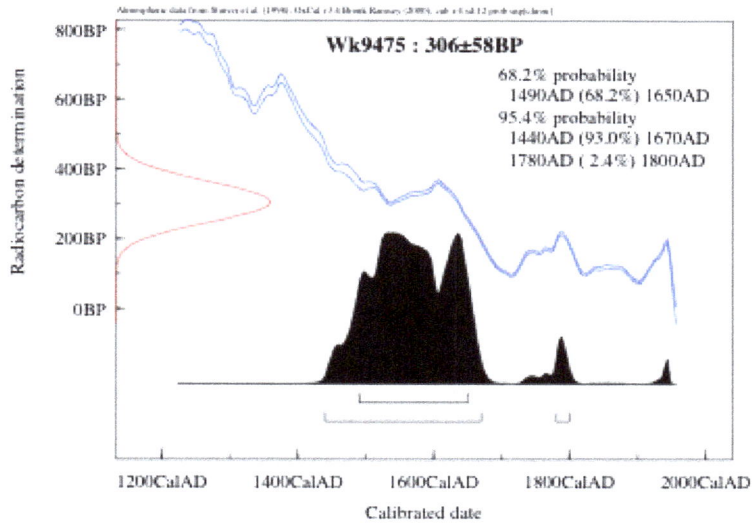

# The University of Waikato
## Radiocarbon Dating Laboratory

Private Bag 3105
Hamilton,
New Zealand.
Fax +64 7 838 4192
Ph +64 7 838 4278
email c14@waikato.ac.nz
Head: Dr Alan Hogg

## Report on Radiocarbon Age Determination for Wk-　　9476

| | |
|---|---|
| **Submitter** | F Beardsley |
| **Submitter's Code** | 48 Unit 4, Level 3 |
| **Site & Location** | Safonfok, Kosrae, Fed States Micronesia, Micronesia |
| **Sample Material** | Shell |
| **Physical Pretreatment** | Surfaces cleaned. Washed in an ultrasonic bath. |
| **Chemical Pretreatment** | Sample acid washed using 5M dil. HCl for 100 seconds, rinsed and dried. |

| | | |
|---|---|---|
| $d^{14}C$ | $-99.2 \pm 4.7$ | ‰ |
| $\delta^{13}C$ | $0.1 \pm 0.2$ | ‰ |
| $D^{14}C$ | $-144.5 \pm 5.5$ | ‰ |
| % Modern | $85.6 \pm 0.5$ | % |
| **Result** | **$1254 \pm 51$ BP** | |

## Comments

*AGHogg*

8/6/01

- Result is *Conventional Age or % Modern* as per Stuiver and Polach, 1977, Radiocarbon 19, 355-363. This is based on the Libby half-life of 5568 yr with correction for isotopic fractionation applied. This age is normally quoted in publications and must include the appropriate error term and Wk number.

- Quoted errors are 1 standard deviation due to counting statistics multiplied by an experimentally determined Laboratory Error Multiplier of 1.217　.

- The isotopic fractionation, $\delta^{13}C$, is expressed as ‰ wrt PDB.

- Results are reported as *% Modern* when the conventional age is younger than 200 yr BP.

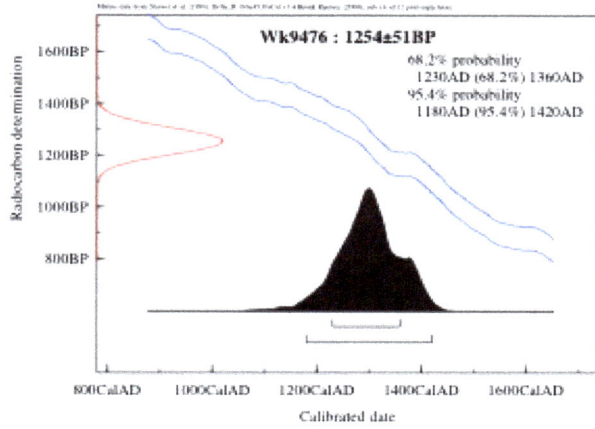

# The University of Waikato
## Radiocarbon Dating Laboratory

Private Bag 3105
Hamilton,
New Zealand.
Fax +64 7 838 4192
Ph +64 7 838 4278
email c14@waikato.ac.nz
Head: Dr Alan Hogg

### Report on Radiocarbon Age Determination for Wk-          9477

| | |
|---|---|
| **Submitter** | F Beardsley |
| **Submitter's Code** | 49 Unit 4, Level 4 |
| **Site & Location** | Safonfok, Kosrae, Fed States Micronesia, Micronesia |
| **Sample Material** | Shell |
| **Physical Pretreatment** | Surfaces cleaned. Washed in an ultrasonic bath. |
| **Chemical Pretreatment** | Sample acid washed using 5 M dil. HCl for 100 seconds, rinsed and dried. |

| | | |
|---|---|---|
| $d^{14}C$ | -64.0 ± 5.0 | ‰ |
| $\delta^{13}C$ | 0.9 ± 0.2 | ‰ |
| $D^{14}C$ | -112.5 ± 5.8 | ‰ |
| % Modern | 88.8 ± 0.6 | % |
| **Result** | **959 ± 52 BP** | |

## Comments

8/6/01

- Result is *Conventional Age or % Modern* as per Stuiver and Polach, 1977, Radiocarbon 19, 355-363. This is based on the Libby half-life of 5568 yr with correction for isotopic fractionation applied. This age is normally quoted in publications and must include the appropriate error term and Wk number.

- Quoted errors are 1 standard deviation due to counting statistics multiplied by an experimentally determined Laboratory Error Multiplier of 1.217 .

- The isotopic fractionation, $\delta^{13}C$, is expressed as ‰ wrt PDB.

- Results are reported as % *Modern* when the conventional age is younger than 200 yr BP.

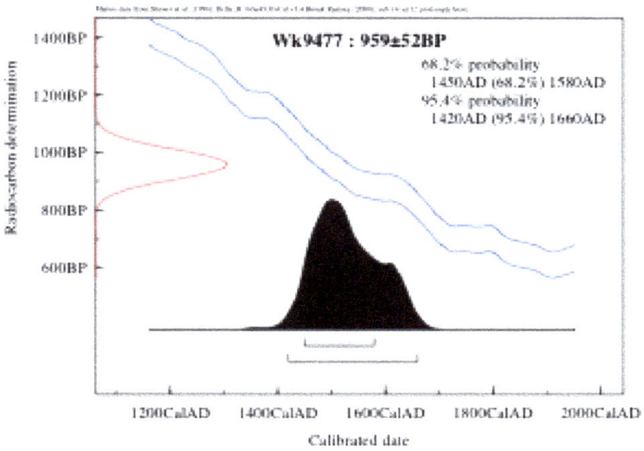
Wk9477 : 959±52BP
68.2% probability
1450AD (68.2%) 1580AD
95.4% probability
1420AD (95.4%) 1660AD
1400BP
1200BP
1000BP
800BP
600BP
Radiocarbon determination
1200CalAD
1400CalAD
1600CalAD
1800CalAD
2000CalAD
Calibrated date

# The University of Waikato
## Radiocarbon Dating Laboratory

Private Bag 3105
Hamilton,
New Zealand.
Fax +64 7 838 4192
Ph +64 7 838 4278
email c14@waikato.ac.nz
Head: Dr Alan Hogg

## Report on Radiocarbon Age Determination for Wk-     9478

| | |
|---|---|
| **Submitter** | F Beardsley |
| **Submitter's Code** | 53 Unit 4, Level 3 |
| **Site & Location** | Safonfok, Kosrae, Fed States Micronesia, Micronesia |
| **Sample Material** | Charcoal |
| **Physical Pretreatment** | Possible contaminants were removed. |
| **Chemical Pretreatment** | Sample washed in hot 10% HCl, rinsed and treated with hot 2% NaOH. The NaOH insoluble fraction was treated with hot 10% HCl, filtered, rinsed and dried. |

| | | |
|---|---|---|
| $d^{14}C$ | $-56.9 \pm 6.8$ | ‰ |
| $\delta^{13}C$ | $-26.2 \pm 0.0$ | ‰ |
| $D^{14}C$ | $-54.6 \pm 8.3$ | ‰ |
| % Modern | $94.5 \pm 0.8$ | % |
| **Result** | **451 ± 71 BP** | |

## Comments

*8/6/01*

- Result is *Conventional Age or % Modern* as per Stuiver and Polach, 1977, Radiocarbon 19, 355-363. This is based on the Libby half-life of 5568 yr with correction for isotopic fractionation applied. This age is normally quoted in publications and must include the appropriate error term and Wk number.

- Quoted errors are 1 standard deviation due to counting statistics multiplied by an experimentally determined Laboratory Error Multiplier of 1.217 .

- The isotopic fractionation, $\delta^{13}C$, is expressed as ‰ wrt PDB.

- Results are reported as *% Modern* when the conventional age is younger than 200 yr BP.

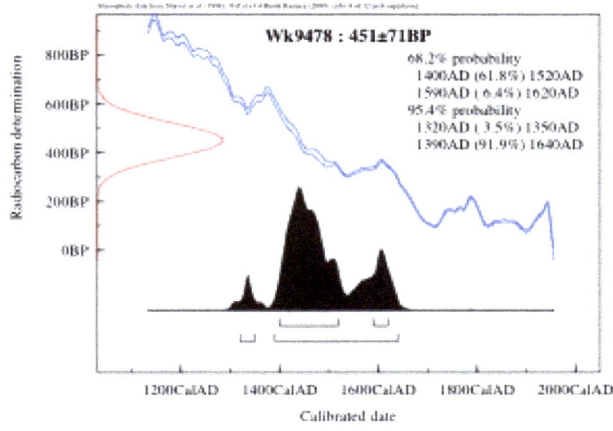

# The University of Waikato
## Radiocarbon Dating Laboratory

Private Bag 3105
Hamilton,
New Zealand.
Fax +64 7 838 4192
Ph +64 7 838 4278
email c14@waikato.ac.nz
Head: Dr Alan Hogg

## Report on Radiocarbon Age Determination for Wk-        9479

( AMS measurement by IGNS [NZA-13688] )

| | |
|---|---|
| **Submitter** | F Beardsley |
| **Submitter's Code** | 55 Unit 4, Level 4 |
| **Site & Location** | Safonfok, Kosrae, Fed States Micronesia, Micronesia |
| **Sample Material** | Charcoal |
| **Physical Pretreatment** | Possible contaminants were removed. |
| **Chemical Pretreatment** | Sample washed in hot 10% HCl, rinsed and treated with hot 2% NaOH. The NaOH insoluble fraction was treated with hot 10% HCl, filtered, rinsed and dried. |

| | | |
|---|---|---|
| $d^{14}C$ | $-50.9 \pm 6.3$ | ‰ |
| $\delta^{13}C$ | $-28.6 \pm 0.2$ | ‰ |
| $D^{14}C$ | $-44.2 \pm 6.4$ | ‰ |
| % Modern | $95.6 \pm 0.6$ | % |
| **Result** | **363 ± 53 BP** | |

## Comments

2/10/01

- Result is *Conventional Age or % Modern* as per Stuiver and Polach, 1977, Radiocarbon 19, 355-363. This is based on the Libby half-life of 5568 yr with correction for isotopic fractionation applied. This age is normally quoted in publications and must include the appropriate error term and Wk number.

- Quoted errors are 1 standard deviation due to counting statistics multiplied by an experimentally determined Laboratory Error Multiplier of 1.

- The isotopic fractionation, $\delta^{13}C$, is expressed as ‰ wrt PDB.

- Results are reported as *% Modern* when the conventional age is younger than 200 yr BP.

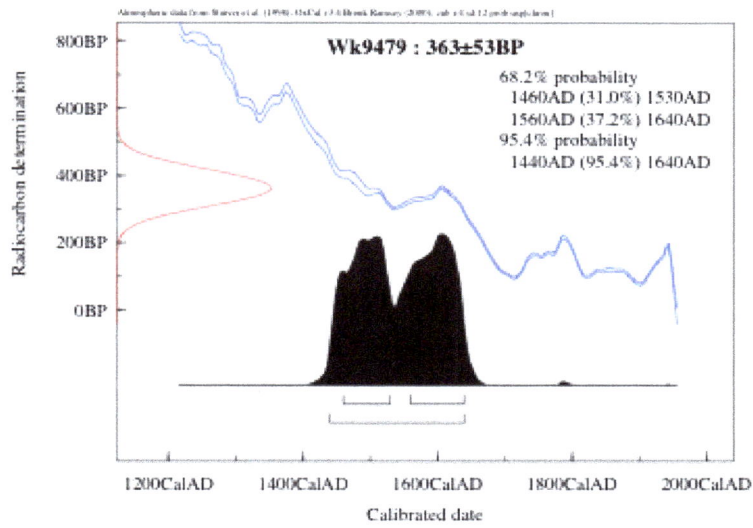

# The University of Waikato
## Radiocarbon Dating Laboratory

Private Bag 3105
Hamilton,
New Zealand.
Fax +64 7 838 4192
Ph +64 7 838 4278
email c14@waikato.ac.nz
Head: Dr Alan Hogg

## Report on Radiocarbon Age Determination for Wk-     9480

| | |
|---|---|
| **Submitter** | F Beardsley |
| **Submitter's Code** | 59 (shell) Unit 4, Level 5 |
| **Site & Location** | Safonfok, Kosrae, Fed States Micronesia, Micronesia |
| **Sample Material** | Shell |
| **Physical Pretreatment** | Surfaces cleaned. Washed in an ultrasonic bath. |
| **Chemical Pretreatment** | Sample acid washed using 5 M dil. HCl for 100 seconds, rinsed and dried. |

| | | |
|---|---|---|
| $d^{14}C$ | $-101.7 \pm 4.8$ | ‰ |
| $\delta^{13}C$ | $0.9 \pm 0.2$ | ‰ |
| $D^{14}C$ | $-148.2 \pm 5.6$ | ‰ |
| % Modern | $85.2 \pm 0.6$ | % |
| **Result** | **$1288 \pm 53$ BP** | |

## Comments

8/6/01

- Result is *Conventional Age or % Modern* as per Stuiver and Polach, 1977, Radiocarbon 19, 355-363. This is based on the Libby half-life of 5568 yr with correction for isotopic fractionation applied. This age is normally quoted in publications and must include the appropriate error term and Wk number.

- Quoted errors are 1 standard deviation due to counting statistics multiplied by an experimentally determined Laboratory Error Multiplier of 1.217 .

- The isotopic fractionation, $\delta^{13}C$, is expressed as ‰ wrt PDB.

- Results are reported as *% Modern* when the conventional age is younger than 200 yr BP.

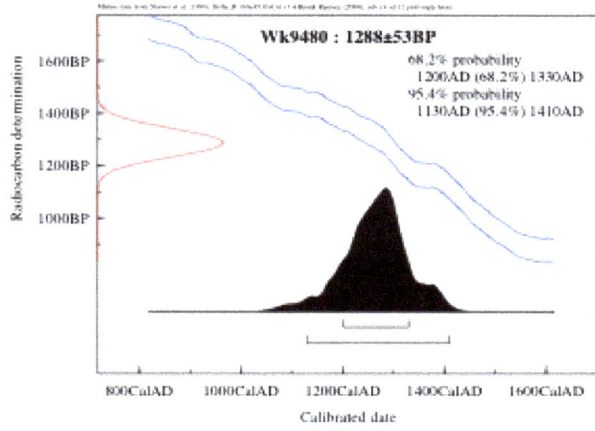

# The University of Waikato
## Radiocarbon Dating Laboratory

Private Bag 3105
Hamilton,
New Zealand.
Fax +64 7 838 4192
Ph +64 7 838 4278
email c14@waikato.ac.nz
Head: Dr Alan Hogg

## Report on Radiocarbon Age Determination for Wk-      9481

( AMS measurement by IGNS [NZA-13562] )

| | |
|---|---|
| **Submitter** | F Beardsley |
| **Submitter's Code** | 59 Unit 4, Level 5 |
| **Site & Location** | Safonfok, Kosrae, Fed States Micronesia, Micronesia |
| **Sample Material** | Charcoal |
| **Physical Pretreatment** | Possible contaminants were removed. |
| **Chemical Pretreatment** | Sample washed in hot 10% HCl, rinsed and treated with hot 2% NaOH. The NaOH insoluble fraction was treated with hot 10% HCl, filtered, rinsed and dried. |

| | | |
|---|---|---|
| $d^{14}C$ | -36.5 ± 6.8 | ‰ |
| $\delta^{13}C$ | -25.1 ± 0.2 | ‰ |
| $D^{14}C$ | -36.2 ± 6.8 | ‰ |
| % Modern | 96.4 ± 0.7 | % |
| **Result** | **297 ± 57 BP** | |

## Comments

*AG Hogg*
13/7/01

- Result is *Conventional Age or % Modern* as per Stuiver and Polach, 1977, Radiocarbon 19, 355-363. This is based on the Libby half-life of 5568 yr with correction for isotopic fractionation applied. This age is normally quoted in publications and must include the appropriate error term and Wk number.

- Quoted errors are 1 standard deviation due to counting statistics multiplied by an experimentally determined Laboratory Error Multiplier of 1.

- The isotopic fractionation, $\delta^{13}C$, is expressed as ‰ wrt PDB.

- Results are reported as *% Modern* when the conventional age is younger than 200 yr BP.

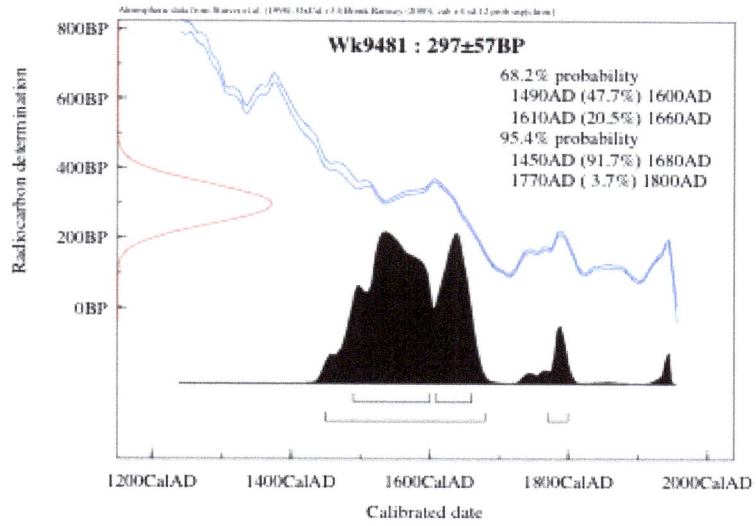

# The University of Waikato
### Radiocarbon Dating Laboratory

Private Bag 3105
Hamilton,
New Zealand.
Fax +64 7 838 4192
Ph +64 7 838 4278
email c14@waikato.ac.nz
Head: Dr Alan Hogg

### Report on Radiocarbon Age Determination for Wk-     9482

| | |
|---|---|
| **Submitter** | F Beardsley |
| **Submitter's Code** | 67 (1) Unit 6, Level 2 |
| **Site & Location** | Safonfok, Kosrae, Fed States Micronesia, Micronesia |
| **Sample Material** | Charcoal |
| **Physical Pretreatment** | Possible contaminants were removed. |
| **Chemical Pretreatment** | Sample washed in hot 10% HCl, rinsed and treated with hot 2% NaOH. The NaOH insoluble fraction was treated with hot 10% HCl, filtered, rinsed and dried. |

| | | |
|---|---|---|
| $d^{14}C$ | -31.4 ± 4.6 | ‰ |
| $\delta^{13}C$ | -26.3 ± 0.0 | ‰ |
| $D^{14}C$ | -28.9 ± 5.6 | ‰ |
| % Modern | 97.1 ± 0.6 | % |
| **Result** | **235 ± 47 BP** | |

## Comments

8/6/01

- Result is *Conventional Age or % Modern* as per Stuiver and Polach, 1977, Radiocarbon 19, 355-363. This is based on the Libby half-life of 5568 yr with correction for isotopic fractionation applied. This age is normally quoted in publications and must include the appropriate error term and Wk number.

- Quoted errors are 1 standard deviation due to counting statistics multiplied by an experimentally determined Laboratory Error Multiplier of 1.217.

- The isotopic fractionation, $\delta^{13}C$, is expressed as ‰ wrt PDB.

- Results are reported as % *Modern* when the conventional age is younger than 200 yr BP.

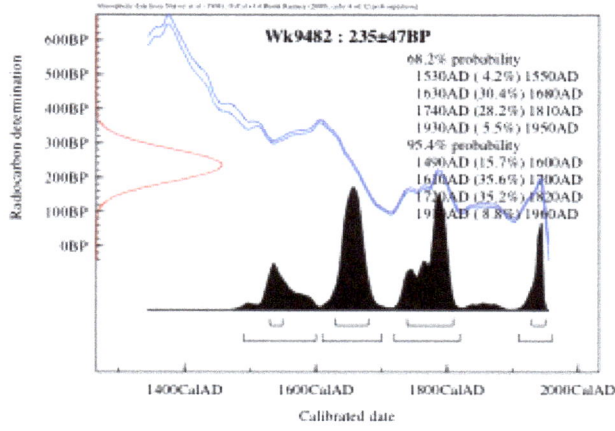

# The University of Waikato
## Radiocarbon Dating Laboratory

Private Bag 3105
Hamilton,
New Zealand.
Fax +64 7 838 4192
Ph +64 7 838 4278
email c14@waikato.ac.nz
Head: Dr Alan Hogg

## Report on Radiocarbon Age Determination for Wk-     9483

| | |
|---|---|
| **Submitter** | F Beardsley |
| **Submitter's Code** | 67 (2) Unit 6, Level 2 |
| **Site & Location** | Safonfok, Kosrae, Fed States Micronesia, Micronesia |
| **Sample Material** | Charcoal |
| **Physical Pretreatment** | Possible contaminants were removed. |

**Chemical Pretreatment**    Sample washed in hot 10% HCl, rinsed and treated with hot 2% NaOH. The NaOH insoluble fraction was treated with hot 10% HCl, filtered, rinsed and dried.

| | | |
|---|---|---|
| $d^{14}C$ | -53.1 ± 5.0 | ‰ |
| $\delta^{13}C$ | -26.8 ± 0.2 | ‰ |
| $D^{14}C$ | -49.6 ± 6.2 | ‰ |
| % Modern | 95.0 ± 0.6 | % |
| **Result** | **409 ± 52 BP** | |

## Comments

*AlHogg*
8/6/01

- Result is *Conventional Age or % Modern* as per Stuiver and Polach, 1977, Radiocarbon 19, 355-363. This is based on the Libby half-life of 5568 yr with correction for isotopic fractionation applied. This age is normally quoted in publications and must include the appropriate error term and Wk number.

- Quoted errors are 1 standard deviation due to counting statistics multiplied by an experimentally determined Laboratory Error Multiplier of 1.217 .

- The isotopic fractionation, $\delta^{13}C$, is expressed as ‰ wrt PDB.

- Results are reported as *% Modern* when the conventional age is younger than 200 yr BP.

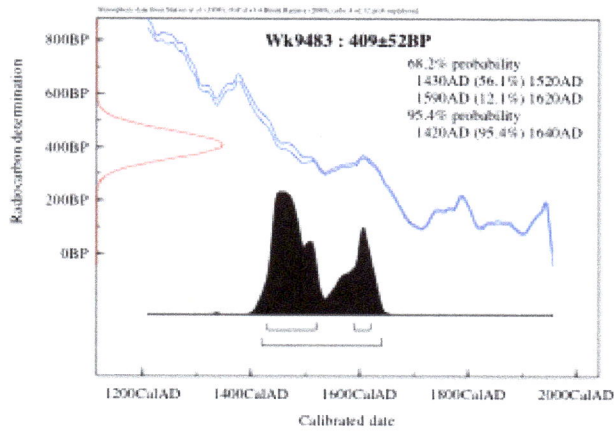

# The University of Waikato
## Radiocarbon Dating Laboratory

Private Bag 3105
Hamilton,
New Zealand.
Fax +64 7 838 4192
Ph +64 7 838 4278
email c14@waikato.ac.nz
Head: Dr Alan Hogg

## Report on Radiocarbon Age Determination for Wk-      9484

| | |
|---|---|
| **Submitter** | F Beardsley |
| **Submitter's Code** | 69 Unit 6, Level 1 |
| **Site & Location** | Safonfok, Kosrae, Fed States Micronesia, Micronesia |
| **Sample Material** | Charcoal |
| **Physical Pretreatment** | Possible contaminants were removed. |
| **Chemical Pretreatment** | Sample washed in hot 10% HCl, rinsed and treated with hot 2% NaOH. The NaOH insoluble fraction was treated with hot 10% HCl, filtered, rinsed and dried. |

| | | |
|---|---|---|
| $d^{14}C$ | $-37.1 \pm 6.4$ | ‰ |
| $\delta^{13}C$ | $-27.3 \pm 0.2$ | ‰ |
| $D^{14}C$ | $-32.8 \pm 7.9$ | ‰ |
| % Modern | $96.7 \pm 0.8$ | % |
| **Result** | **$268 \pm 66$ BP** | |

## Comments

8/6/01

- Result is *Conventional Age or % Modern* as per Stuiver and Polach, 1977, Radiocarbon 19, 355-363. This is based on the Libby half-life of 5568 yr with correction for isotopic fractionation applied. This age is normally quoted in publications and must include the appropriate error term and Wk number.

- Quoted errors are 1 standard deviation due to counting statistics multiplied by an experimentally determined Laboratory Error Multiplier of 1.217 .

- The isotopic fractionation, $\delta^{13}C$, is expressed as ‰ wrt PDB.

- Results are reported as *% Modern* when the conventional age is younger than 200 yr BP.

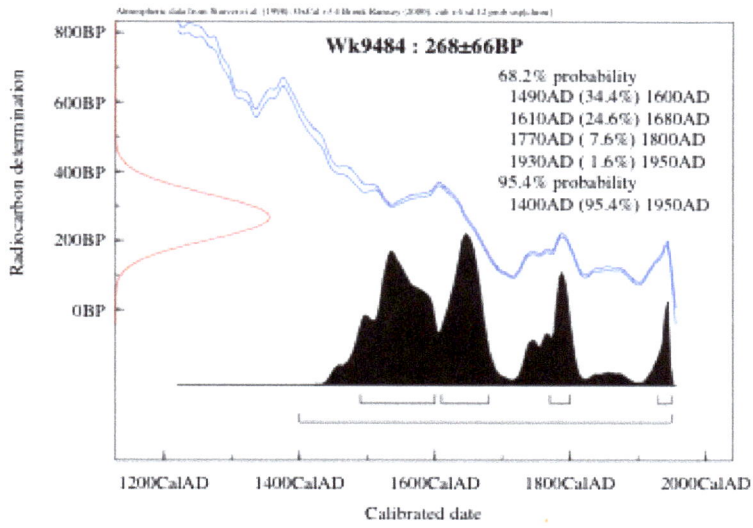

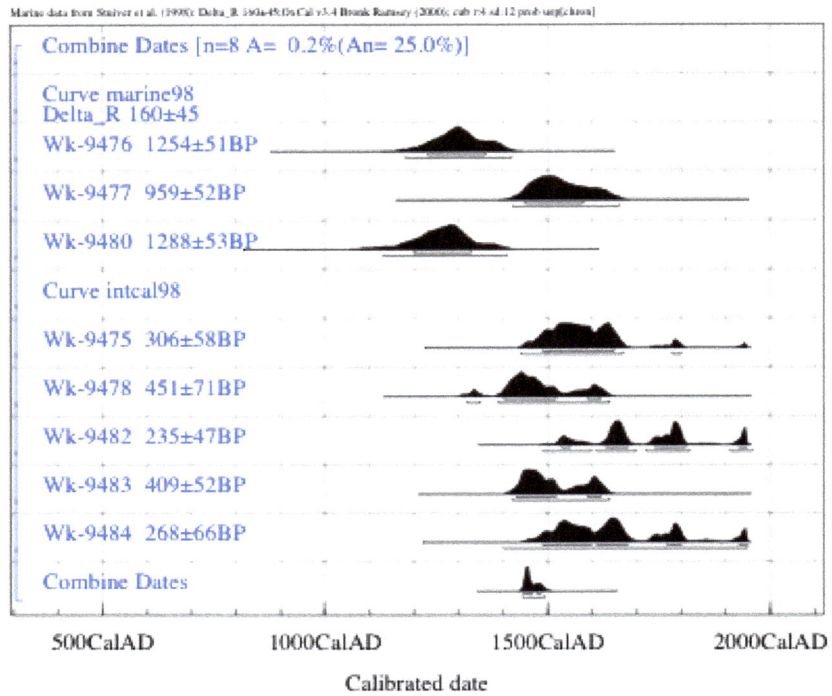

Marine data from Stuiver et al. (1998); Delta_R 160±45; OxCal v3.4 Bronk Ramsey (2000); cub r:4 sd:12 prob-usp[chron]

Combine Dates [n=8 A= 0.2%(An= 25.0%)]

Curve marine98
Delta_R 160±45
Wk-9476 1254±51BP

Wk-9477 959±52BP

Wk-9480 1288±53BP

Curve intcal98

Wk-9475 306±58BP

Wk-9478 451±71BP

Wk-9482 235±47BP

Wk-9483 409±52BP

Wk-9484 268±66BP

Combine Dates

500CalAD          1000CalAD          1500CalAD          2000CalAD

Calibrated date

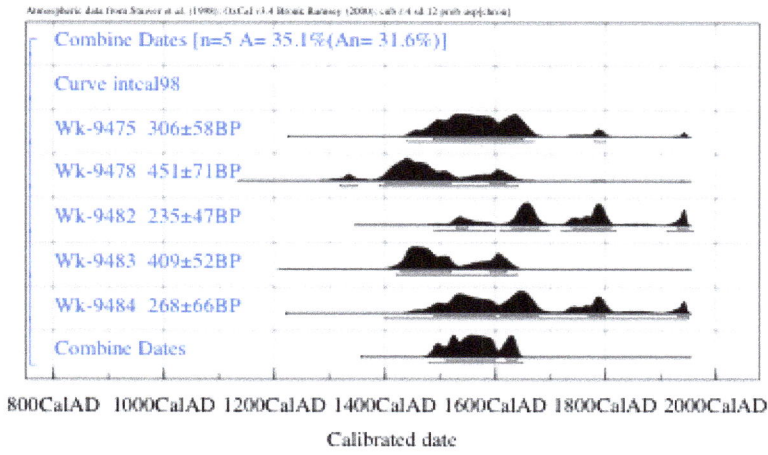

Atmospheric data from Stuiver et al. (1998); OxCal v3.4 Bronk Ramsey (2000); cub r:4 sd:12 prob usp[chron]

Combine Dates [n=5 A= 35.1%{An= 31.6%)]

Curve intcal98

Wk-9475  306±58BP

Wk-9478  451±71BP

Wk-9482  235±47BP

Wk-9483  409±52BP

Wk-9484  268±66BP

Combine Dates

800CalAD  1000CalAD 1200CalAD 1400CalAD 1600CalAD 1800CalAD 2000CalAD

Calibrated date

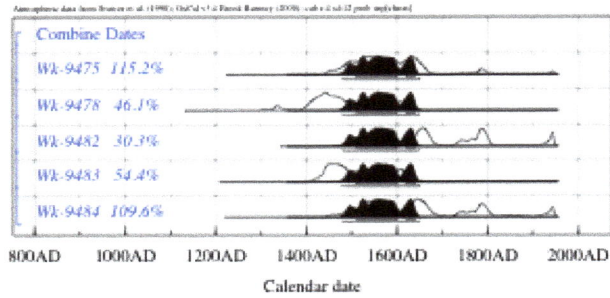

# The University of Waikato
## Radiocarbon Dating Laboratory

Private Bag 3105
Hamilton,
New Zealand.
Fax +64 7 838 4192
Ph +64 7 838 4278
email c14@waikato.ac.nz
Head: Dr Alan Hogg

### Report on Radiocarbon Age Determination for Wk-   11829

| | |
|---|---|
| **Submitter** | F Beardsley |
| **Submitter's Code** | 94 |
| **Site & Location** | Southwest coast of Kosrae Island, Micronesia, Federated States o |
| **Sample Material** | Charcoal |
| **Physical Pretreatment** | Possible contaminants were removed. Washed in ultrasonic bath. |
| **Chemical Pretreatment** | Sample washed in hot 10% HCl, rinsed and treated with hot 0.5% NaOH. The NaOH insoluble fraction was treated with hot 10% HCl, filtered, rinsed and dried. |

| | | |
|---|---|---|
| $d^{14}C$ | $-43.4 \pm 4.5$ | ‰ |
| $\delta^{13}C$ | $-25.5 \pm 0.2$ | ‰ |
| $D^{14}C$ | $-42.4 \pm 5.5$ | ‰ |
| % Modern | $95.8 \pm 0.6$ | % |
| **Result** | **348 ± 46 BP** | |

## Comments

29/01/03

- Result is *Conventional Age or % Modern* as per Stuiver and Polach, 1977, Radiocarbon 19, 355-363. This is based on the Libby half-life of 5568 yr with correction for isotopic fractionation applied. This age is normally quoted in publications and must include the appropriate error term and Wk number.

- Quoted errors are 1 standard deviation due to counting statistics multiplied by an experimentally determined Laboratory Error Multiplier of 1.217 .

- The isotopic fractionation, $\delta^{13}C$, is expressed as ‰ wrt PDB.

- Results are reported as *% Modern* when the conventional age is younger than 200 yr BP.

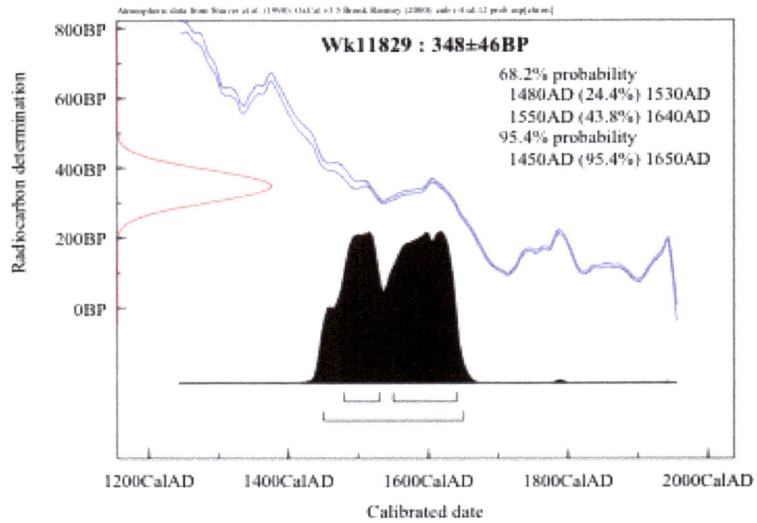

# The University of Waikato
### Radiocarbon Dating Laboratory

Private Bag 3105
Hamilton,
New Zealand.
Fax +64 7 838 4192
Ph +64 7 838 4278
email c14@waikato.ac.nz
Head: Dr Alan Hogg

## Report on Radiocarbon Age Determination for Wk-    *11830*
( AMS measurement by IGNS [NZA-16441] )

| | |
|---|---|
| **Submitter** | F Beardsley |
| **Submitter's Code** | 180 |
| **Site & Location** | Southwest coast of Kosrae Island, Micronesia, Federated States o |
| **Sample Material** | Charcoal |
| **Physical Pretreatment** | Possible contaminants were removed. Washed in ultrasonic bath. |
| **Chemical Pretreatment** | Sample washed in hot 10% HCl, rinsed and treated with hot 1% NaOH. The NaOH insoluble fraction was treated with hot 10% HCl, filtered, rinsed and dried. |

| | | |
|---|---|---|
| $d^{14}C$ | -36.0 ± 5.0 | ‰ |
| $\delta^{13}C$ | -26.6 ± 0.2 | ‰ |
| $D^{14}C$ | -36.7 ± 5.1 | ‰ |
| % Modern | 96.3 ± 0.5 | % |
| **Result** | **300 ± 43 BP** | |

## Comments

*AlHogg*
29/01/03

- Result is *Conventional Age or % Modern* as per Stuiver and Polach, 1977, Radiocarbon 19, 355-363. This is based on the Libby half-life of 5568 yr with correction for isotopic fractionation applied. This age is normally quoted in publications and must include the appropriate error term and Wk number.

- Quoted errors are 1 standard deviation due to counting statistics multiplied by an experimentally determined Laboratory Error Multiplier of 1 .

- The isotopic fractionation, $\delta^{13}C$, is expressed as ‰ wrt PDB.

- Results are reported as *% Modern* when the conventional age is younger than 200 yr BP.

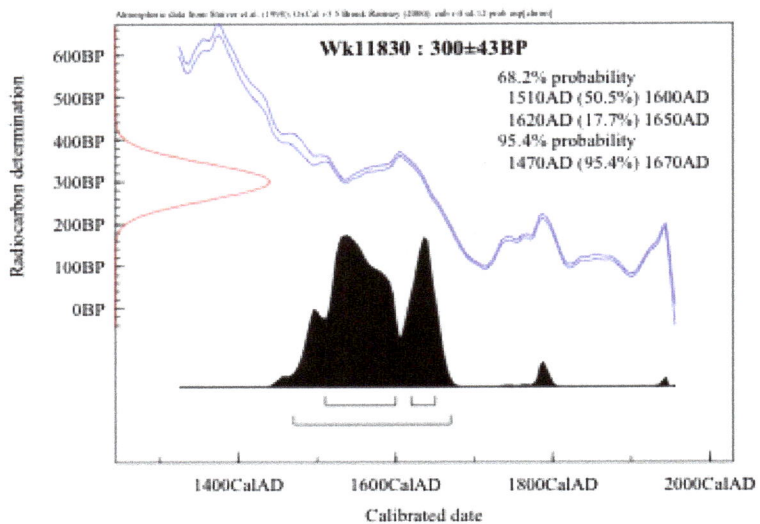

# The University of Waikato
## Radiocarbon Dating Laboratory

Private Bag 3105
Hamilton,
New Zealand.
Fax +64 7 838 4192
Ph +64 7 838 4278
email c14@waikato.ac.nz
Head: Dr Alan Hogg

## Report on Radiocarbon Age Determination for Wk-          11831

| | |
|---|---|
| **Submitter** | F Beardsley |
| **Submitter's Code** | 197 |
| **Site & Location** | Southwest coast of Kosrae Island, Micronesia, Federated States o |
| **Sample Material** | Charcoal |
| **Physical Pretreatment** | Possible contaminants were removed. Washed in ultrasonic bath. |
| **Chemical Pretreatment** | Sample washed in hot 10% HCl, rinsed and treated with hot 0.5% NaOH. The NaOH insoluble fraction was treated with hot 10% HCl, filtered, rinsed and dried. |

| | | |
|---|---|---|
| $d^{14}C$ | $-45.8 \pm 4.7$ | ‰ |
| $\delta^{13}C$ | $-26.0 \pm 0.2$ | ‰ |
| $D^{14}C$ | $-43.8 \pm 5.7$ | ‰ |
| % Modern | $95.6 \pm 0.6$ | % |
| **Result** | **359 ± 49 BP** | |

## Comments

29/01/03

- Result is *Conventional Age or % Modern* as per Stuiver and Polach, 1977, Radiocarbon 19, 355-363. This is based on the Libby half-life of 5568 yr with correction for isotopic fractionation applied. This age is normally quoted in publications and must include the appropriate error term and Wk number.

- Quoted errors are 1 standard deviation due to counting statistics multiplied by an experimentally determined Laboratory Error Multiplier of 1.217 .

- The isotopic fractionation, $\delta^{13}C$, is expressed as ‰ wrt PDB.

- Results are reported as % *Modern* when the conventional age is younger than 200 yr BP.

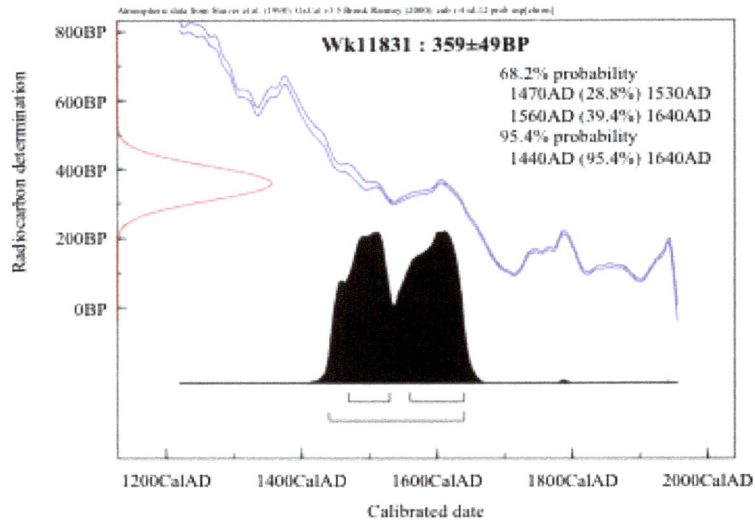

# The University of Waikato
## Radiocarbon Dating Laboratory

Private Bag 3105
Hamilton,
New Zealand.
Fax +64 7 838 4192
Ph +64 7 838 4278
email c14@waikato.ac.nz
Head: Dr Alan Hogg

## Report on Radiocarbon Age Determination for Wk-    *11832*

( AMS measurement by IGNS [NZA-16442] )

| | |
|---|---|
| **Submitter** | F Beardsley |
| **Submitter's Code** | 198 |
| **Site & Location** | Southwest coast of Kosrae Island, Micronesia, Federated States o |
| **Sample Material** | Charcoal |
| **Physical Pretreatment** | Possible contaminants were removed. Washed in ultrasonic bath. |
| **Chemical Pretreatment** | Sample washed in hot 10% HCl, rinsed and treated with hot 0.5% NaOH. The NaOH insoluble fraction was treated with hot 10% HCl, filtered, rinsed and dried. |

| | | |
|---|---|---|
| $d^{14}C$ | -52.4 ± 4.7 | ‰ |
| $\delta^{13}C$ | -25.9 ± 0.2 | ‰ |
| $D^{14}C$ | -54.5 ± 4.8 | ‰ |
| % Modern | 94.6 ± 0.5 | % |
| **Result** | **450 ± 41 BP** | |

## Comments

29/01/03

- Result is *Conventional Age or % Modern* as per Stuiver and Polach, 1977, Radiocarbon 19, 355-363. This is based on the Libby half-life of 5568 yr with correction for isotopic fractionation applied. This age is normally quoted in publications and must include the appropriate error term and Wk number.

- Quoted errors are 1 standard deviation due to counting statistics multiplied by an experimentally determined Laboratory Error Multiplier of 1.

- The isotopic fractionation, $\delta^{13}C$, is expressed as ‰ wrt PDB.

- Results are reported as % *Modern* when the conventional age is younger than 200 yr BP.

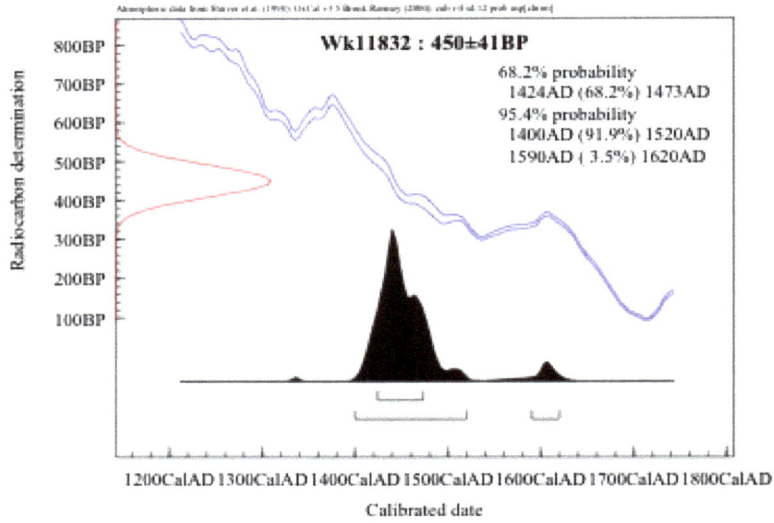

# The University of Waikato
## Radiocarbon Dating Laboratory

Private Bag 3105
Hamilton,
New Zealand.
Fax +64 7 838 4192
Ph +64 7 838 4278
email c14@waikato.ac.nz
Head: Dr Alan Hogg

## Report on Radiocarbon Age Determination for Wk-    11833

( AMS measurement by IGNS [NZA-16443] )

| | |
|---|---|
| **Submitter** | F Beardsley |
| **Submitter's Code** | 199 |
| **Site & Location** | Southwest coast of Kosrae Island, Micronesia, Federated States o |
| **Sample Material** | Charcoal |
| **Physical Pretreatment** | Possible contaminants were removed. Washed in ultrasonic bath. |
| **Chemical Pretreatment** | Sample washed in hot 10% HCl, rinsed and treated with hot 0.5% NaOH. The NaOH insoluble fraction was treated with hot 10% HCl, filtered, rinsed and dried. |

| | | |
|---|---|---|
| $d^{14}C$ | $-40.3 \pm 4.7$ | ‰ |
| $\delta^{13}C$ | $-24.8 \pm 0.2$ | ‰ |
| $D^{14}C$ | $-44.5 \pm 4.8$ | ‰ |
| % Modern | $95.6 \pm 0.5$ | % |
| **Result** | **365 ± 41 BP** | |

## Comments

29/01/03

- Result is *Conventional Age or % Modern* as per Stuiver and Polach, 1977, Radiocarbon 19, 355-363. This is based on the Libby half-life of 5568 yr with correction for isotopic fractionation applied. This age is normally quoted in publications and must include the appropriate error term and Wk number.

- Quoted errors are 1 standard deviation due to counting statistics multiplied by an experimentally determined Laboratory Error Multiplier of 1.

- The isotopic fractionation, $\delta^{13}C$, is expressed as ‰ wrt PDB.

- Results are reported as *% Modern* when the conventional age is younger than 200 yr BP.

107

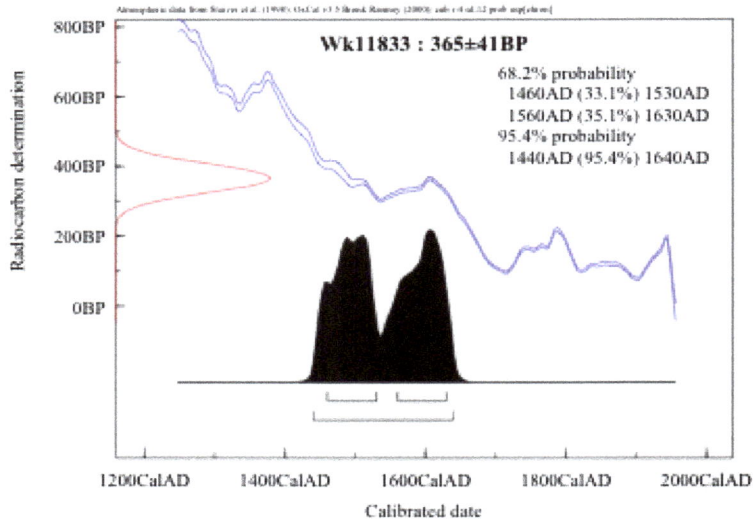

# The University of Waikato
## Radiocarbon Dating Laboratory

Private Bag 3105
Hamilton,
New Zealand.
Fax +64 7 838 4192
Ph +64 7 838 4278
email c14@waikato.ac.nz
Head: Dr Alan Hogg

## Report on Radiocarbon Age Determination for Wk-      *11834*

( AMS measurement by IGNS [NZA-16444] )

| | |
|---|---|
| **Submitter** | F Beardsley |
| **Submitter's Code** | 200 |
| **Site & Location** | Southwest coast of Kosrae Island, Micronesia, Federated States o |
| **Sample Material** | Charcoal |
| **Physical Pretreatment** | Possible contaminants were removed. Washed in ultrasonic bath. |
| **Chemical Pretreatment** | Sample washed in hot 10% HCl, rinsed and treated with hot 0.5% NaOH. The NaOH insoluble fraction was treated with hot 10% HCl, filtered, rinsed and dried. |

| | | |
|---|---|---|
| $d^{14}C$ | $-49.1 \pm 4.7$ | ‰ |
| $\delta^{13}C$ | $-25.4 \pm 0.2$ | ‰ |
| $D^{14}C$ | $-52.1 \pm 4.8$ | ‰ |
| % Modern | $94.8 \pm 0.5$ | % |
| **Result** | **430 ± 41 BP** | |

## Comments

*AliHogg*
29/01/03

- Result is *Conventional Age or % Modern* as per Stuiver and Polach, 1977, Radiocarbon 19, 355-363. This is based on the Libby half-life of 5568 yr with correction for isotopic fractionation applied. This age is normally quoted in publications and must include the appropriate error term and Wk number.

- Quoted errors are 1 standard deviation due to counting statistics multiplied by an experimentally determined Laboratory Error Multiplier of 1 .

- The isotopic fractionation. $\delta^{13}C$, is expressed as ‰ wrt PDB.

- Results are reported as *% Modern* when the conventional age is younger than 200 yr BP.

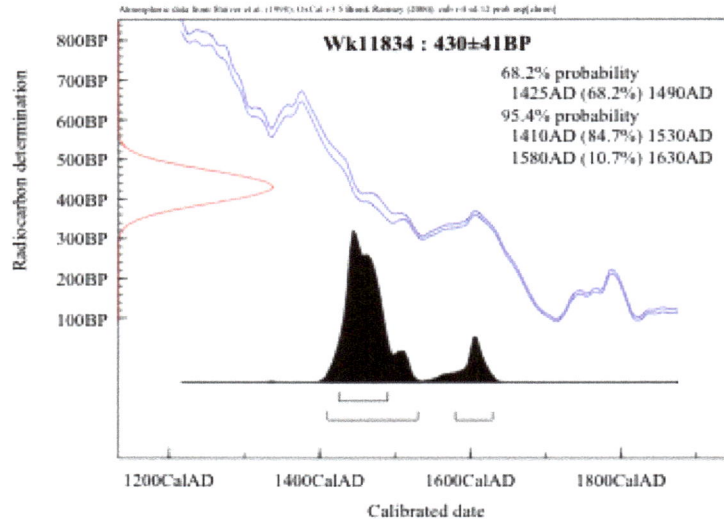

# The University of Waikato
## Radiocarbon Dating Laboratory

Private Bag 3105
Hamilton,
New Zealand.
Fax +64 7 838 4192
Ph +64 7 838 4278
email c14@waikato.ac.nz
Head: Dr Alan Hogg

## Report on Radiocarbon Age Determination for Wk-    11835

| | |
|---|---|
| **Submitter** | F Beardsley |
| **Submitter's Code** | 211 |
| **Site & Location** | Southwest coast of Kosrae Island, Micronesia, Federated States o |
| **Sample Material** | Charcoal |
| **Physical Pretreatment** | Possible contaminants were removed. Washed in ultrasonic bath. |
| **Chemical Pretreatment** | Sample washed in hot 10% HCl, rinsed and treated with hot 0.5% NaOH. The NaOH insoluble fraction was treated with hot 10% HCl, filtered, rinsed and dried. |

| | | |
|---|---|---|
| $d^{14}C$ | $-78.2 \pm 7.4$ | ‰ |
| $\delta^{13}C$ | $-26.0 \pm 0.2$ | ‰ |
| $D^{14}C$ | $-76.4 \pm 9.1$ | ‰ |
| % Modern | $92.4 \pm 0.9$ | % |
| **Result** | **639 ± 79 BP** | |

## Comments

*ALHogg*
29/01/03

- Result is *Conventional Age or % Modern* as per Stuiver and Polach, 1977, Radiocarbon 19, 355-363. This is based on the Libby half-life of 5568 yr with correction for isotopic fractionation applied. This age is normally quoted in publications and must include the appropriate error term and Wk number.

- Quoted errors are 1 standard deviation due to counting statistics multiplied by an experimentally determined Laboratory Error Multiplier of 1.217 .

- The isotopic fractionation, $\delta^{13}C$, is expressed as ‰ wrt PDB.

- Results are reported as *% Modern* when the conventional age is younger than 200 yr BP.

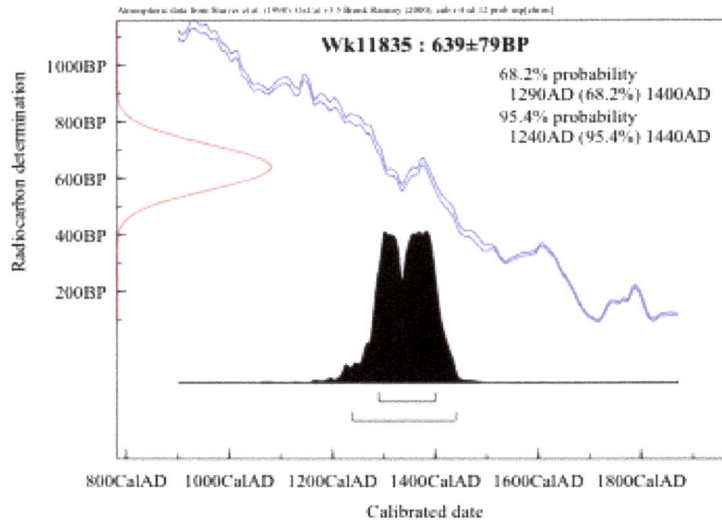

# The University of Waikato
## Radiocarbon Dating Laboratory

Private Bag 3105
Hamilton,
New Zealand.
Fax +64 7 838 4192
Ph +64 7 838 4278
email c14@waikato.ac.nz
Head: Dr Alan Hogg

## Report on Radiocarbon Age Determination for Wk-      11836

| | |
|---|---|
| **Submitter** | F Beardsley |
| **Submitter's Code** | 212 |
| **Site & Location** | Southwest coast of Kosrae Island, Micronesia, Federated States o |
| **Sample Material** | Charcoal |
| **Physical Pretreatment** | Possible contaminants were removed. Washed in ultrasonic bath. |
| **Chemical Pretreatment** | Sample washed in hot 10% HCl, rinsed and treated with hot 0.5% NaOH. The NaOH insoluble fraction was treated with hot 10% HCl, filtered, rinsed and dried. |

| | | |
|---|---|---|
| $d^{14}C$ | $-55.0 \pm 4.9$ | ‰ |
| $\delta^{13}C$ | $-25.7 \pm 0.2$ | ‰ |
| $D^{14}C$ | $-53.7 \pm 5.9$ | ‰ |
| % Modern | $94.6 \pm 0.6$ | % |
| **Result** | $443 \pm 51$ BP | |

## Comments

*AliHogg*

29/01/03

- Result is *Conventional Age or % Modern* as per Stuiver and Polach, 1977, Radiocarbon 19, 355-363. This is based on the Libby half-life of 5568 yr with correction for isotopic fractionation applied. This age is normally quoted in publications and must include the appropriate error term and Wk number.

- Quoted errors are 1 standard deviation due to counting statistics multiplied by an experimentally determined Laboratory Error Multiplier of 1.217 .

- The isotopic fractionation. $\delta^{13}C$, is expressed as ‰ wrt PDB.

- Results are reported as % *Modern* when the conventional age is younger than 200 yr BP.

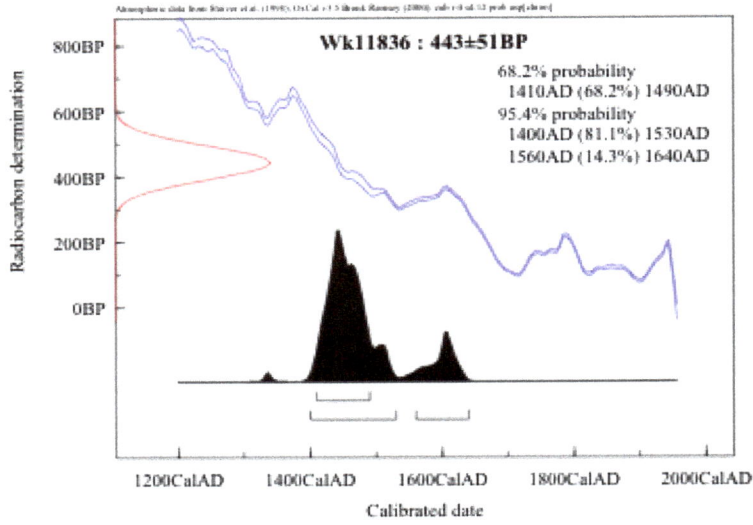

# The University of Waikato
## Radiocarbon Dating Laboratory

Private Bag 3105
Hamilton,
New Zealand.
Fax +64 7 838 4192
Ph +64 7 838 4278
email c14@waikato.ac.nz
Head: Dr Alan Hogg

## *Report on Radiocarbon Age Determination for Wk-*     *11837*

| | |
|---|---|
| **Submitter** | F Beardsley |
| **Submitter's Code** | 440 |
| **Site & Location** | Southwest coast of Kosrae Island, Micronesia, Federated States o |
| | |
| **Sample Material** | Charcoal |
| **Physical Pretreatment** | Possible contaminants were removed. Washed in ultrasonic bath. |
| | |
| **Chemical Pretreatment** | Sample washed in hot 10% HCl, rinsed and treated with hot 0.5% NaOH. The NaOH insoluble fraction was treated with hot 10% HCl, filtered, rinsed and dried. |

| | | |
|---|---|---|
| $d^{14}C$ | -50.3 ± 5.1 | ‰ |
| $\delta^{13}C$ | -25.7 ± 0.2 | ‰ |
| $D^{14}C$ | -49.0 ± 6.2 | ‰ |
| % Modern | 95.1 ± 0.6 | % |
| **Result** | **404 ± 52 BP** | |

## Comments

*29/01/03*

---

- Result is *Conventional Age or % Modern* as per Stuiver and Polach, 1977, Radiocarbon 19, 355-363. This is based on the Libby half-life of 5568 yr with correction for isotopic fractionation applied. This age is normally quoted in publications and must include the appropriate error term and Wk number.

- Quoted errors are 1 standard deviation due to counting statistics multiplied by an experimentally determined Laboratory Error Multiplier of 1.217 .

- The isotopic fractionation, $\delta^{13}C$, is expressed as ‰ wrt PDB.

- Results are reported as *% Modern* when the conventional age is younger than 200 yr BP.

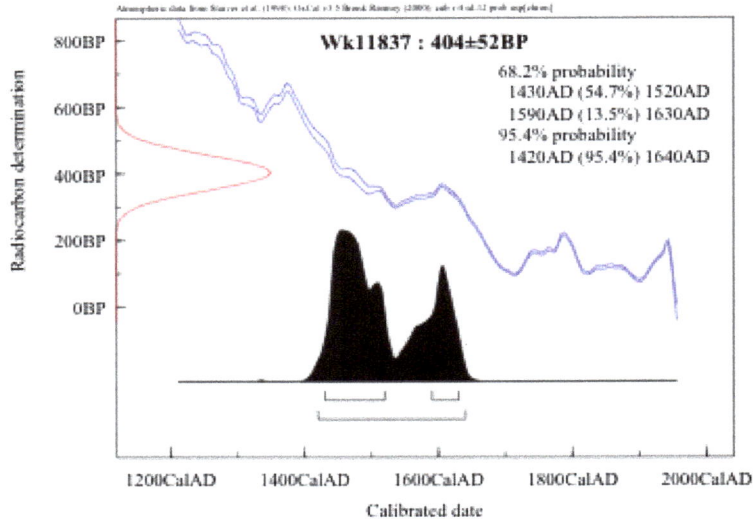

Wk11837 : 404±52BP

68.2% probability
1430AD (54.7%) 1520AD
1590AD (13.5%) 1630AD
95.4% probability
1420AD (95.4%) 1640AD

# The University of Waikato
## Radiocarbon Dating Laboratory

Private Bag 3105
Hamilton,
New Zealand.
Fax +64 7 838 4192
Ph +64 7 838 4278
email c14@waikato.ac.nz
Head: Dr Alan Hogg

## Report on Radiocarbon Age Determination for Wk-        11838

| | |
|---|---|
| **Submitter** | F Beardsley |
| **Submitter's Code** | 463 |
| **Site & Location** | Southwest coast of Kosrae Island, Micronesia, Federated States o |
| **Sample Material** | Charcoal |
| **Physical Pretreatment** | Possible contaminants were removed. Washed in ultrasonic bath. |
| **Chemical Pretreatment** | Sample washed in hot 10% HCl, rinsed and treated with hot 0.5% NaOH. The NaOH insoluble fraction was treated with hot 10% HCl, filtered, rinsed and dried. |

| | | |
|---|---|---|
| $d^{14}C$ | -32.7 ± 4.7 | ‰ |
| $\delta^{13}C$ | -26.7 ± 0.2 | ‰ |
| $D^{14}C$ | -29.3 ± 5.7 | ‰ |
| % Modern | 97.1 ± 0.6 | % |
| **Result** | **239 ± 48 BP** | |

## Comments

*AliHogg*

29/01/03

- Result is *Conventional Age or % Modern* as per Stuiver and Polach, 1977, Radiocarbon 19, 355-363. This is based on the Libby half-life of 5568 yr with correction for isotopic fractionation applied. This age is normally quoted in publications and must include the appropriate error term and Wk number.

- Quoted errors are 1 standard deviation due to counting statistics multiplied by an experimentally determined Laboratory Error Multiplier of 1.217 .

- The isotopic fractionation, $\delta^{13}C$, is expressed as ‰ wrt PDB.

- Results are reported as *% Modern* when the conventional age is younger than 200 yr BP.

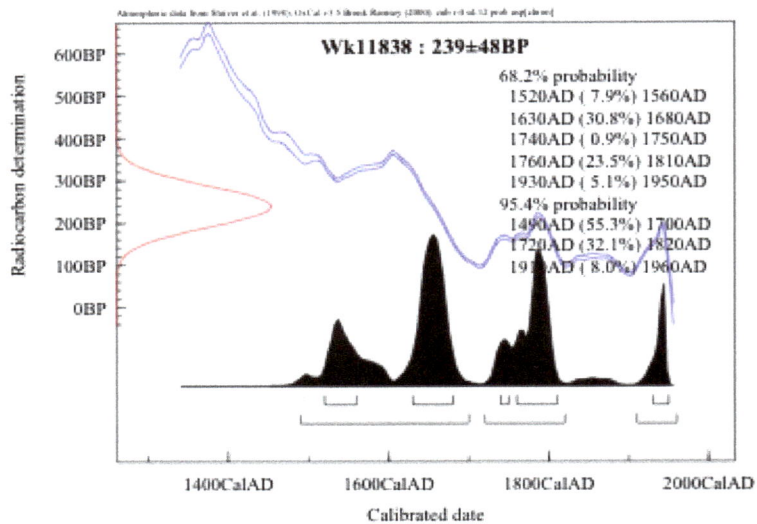

www.ingramcontent.com/pod-product-compliance
Lightning Source LLC
Chambersburg PA
CBHW06  002030426
42334CB00033B/3335